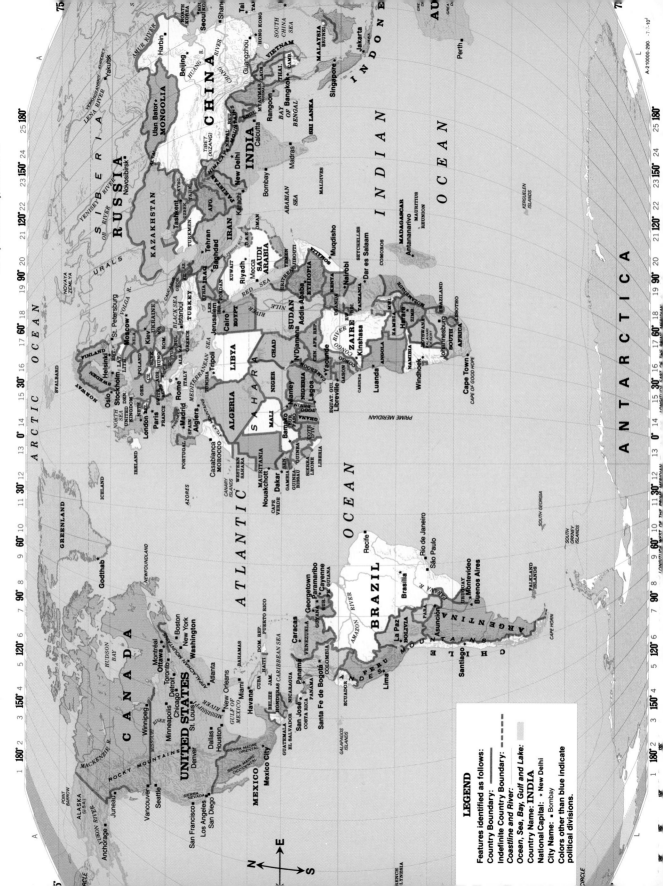

From Classroom Atlas: 1994 Edition
© 1994 by Rand McNally, R.L. 94-S-13

6100 20 000

ÎLES TUAMOTU
(Fr.)

SANTIAGO
ARGENTINA
BRASILIA

ARCH.
DE LOS
CHONOS

CHILE

Rosario

URUGUAY

BUENOS
AIRES
MONTEVIDEO
Santos

RIO DE
JANEIRO

SÃO
PAULO

Punta Arenas

Estr. de
Magallanes
FALKLAND IS.
(ISLAS MALVINAS)
(Br.)
CABO DE HORNOS

Drake Passage

SOUTH SHETLAND
ISLANDS (B.A.T.)

BELLINGSHAUSEN

ADELAIDE

SOUTH
ORKNEY IS.
(B.A.T.)

SOUTH GEORGIA
(Falkland Is.)

SOUTH
SANDWICH IS.
(Falkland Is.)

GOUGH
(Br.)

TRISTAN DA
CUNHA
(Br.)

Antarctic Circle

AMUNDSEN

THURSTON I.

ALEXANDER I.

Mt. Rex
3 625

Mt. Siple
10 171
Mt. Ulmer
8 451
ELLSWORTH
MTS.
EXECUTIVE
COMMITTEE
RANGE
Mt. Sidley
13 717
Vinson
Massif
16 066
WHITMORE
MTS.
ROCKEFELLER
PLATEAU
THIEL
MTS.
Mt. Hogg
1 503
PENSACOLA
MTS.

RONNE
ICE SHELF
BERKNER
ISLAND
FILCHNER ICE SHELF
COATS
LAND

WADDELL
SEA

BOUVETØYA
(Nor.)

Little America
ROOSEVELT I.
SCOTT
ROSS
ICE SHELF
HORLICK
MTS.
QUEEN
MAUD
MTS.
South Pole
10 000
QUEEN
MAUD
LAND
MÜHLIG
HOFMANN
MTS.

Mt. Erebus
12 280
McMurdo
Mt. Markham
14 275
Mt. Albert Markham
10 522
Mt. McClintock 11 457
SØR
RONDANE
MTS.
BELGICA MTS.

C. OF GOOD HOPE
Cape Town

AFRICA

Mt. Sabine
12 201
ROSS
SEA
BALLENY IS.
VICTORIA
LAND
ANTARCTICA
80°
QUEEN FABIOLA
MTS.

NEW
ZEALAND
CHATHAM IS.
(N.Z.)
BOUNTY IS.
(N.Z.)
CAMPBELL I.
(N.Z.)
AUCKLAND IS.
(N.Z.)

South
Magnetic Pole
WILKES
LAND
AMERICAN
HIGHLAND
NAPIER MTS.
ENDERBY
LAND
Antarctic Circle

SOUTH
AFRICA
LESOTHO
SWAZILAND
Durban
MOZAMBIQUE

MACQUARIE
(Austl.)

SHACKLETON ICE SHELF

PRINCE
EDWARD IS.
(S. Africa)

TASMAN
SEA

Hobart
TASMANIA

HEARD
(Austl.)
McDONALD
(Austl.)
ÎLES CROZET
(Fr.)

MELBOURNE

ÎLES KERGUÉLEN
(Fr.)

C. STE. MARIE

MADAGASCAR

Adelaide

AUSTRALIA

GREAT VICTORIA
DESERT
C. LEEUWIN
Perth

C. D'AMBRE
COMORO

GREAT
SANDY
DESERT

Antananarivo

RÉUNION
(Fr.)
MASCARENE IS.
MAURITIUS

ÎLE AMSTERDAM
(Fr.)
ÎLE ST-PAUL
(Fr.)

Tropic of Capricorn

TIMOR SEA
TIMOR
FLORES
INDONESIA

NORTH WEST
CAPE

AMIRANTE IS.
(Sey.)

SEYCHELLES

INDIAN

OCEAN

ANTARCTICA IN PROFILE
SECTION ALONG LINE AB

South Pole
15000
10000
5000
Feet (A)
Sea Level
5000

Horlick Mts.
Byrd Basin
Polar Basin
Sea Level
Framnes
Mts.
15000
10000
5000
(B) Feet
5000

Map from Goode's World Atlas
©1994 by Rand McNally, R.L. 94-S-13

Scale 1: 60 000 000; (approximate)
Lambert's Azimuthal, Equal Area Projection
Elevations and depressions are given in feet

Enchantment of the World

ANTARCTICA

By Henry Billings

Consultants for Antarctica: Debra J. Enzenbacher, Ph.D. Candidate, Scott Polar Research Institute, University of Cambridge, Cambridge, England; Beth C. Marks, M.S., Director, The Antarctica Project, Washington, D.C.

Consultant for Reading: Robert L. Hillerich, Ph. D., Professor Emeritus, Bowling Green State University; Consultant, Pinellas County Schools, Florida

 CHILDRENS PRESS®
CHICAGO

Adélie penguins live on the shores of Antarctica and its islands.

Project Editor: Mary Reidy
Design: Margrit Fiddle

Library of Congress Cataloging-in-Publication Data

Billings, Henry.
   Antarctica / by Henry Billings.
      p.   cm. – (Enchantment of the world)
   Includes index.
   Summary: Discusses the location, climate, plant and
animal life, discovery and exploration, and the cooperation
of nations in preserving the fifth-largest continent.
   ISBN 0-516-02624-0
   1. Antarctica–Juvenile literature.   [1. Antarctica.]
I. Title. II. Series.
G863.B55 1994   94-9142
998.9–dc20   CIP
                                                           AC

Picture Acknowledgments
AP/Wide World Photos: 78 (right), 79, 81 (left), 83 (left);
© **Knoedler Galleries, NY City,** 9 (right)
The Bettmann Archive: 8 (2 photos), 10 (left & center), 53
(2 photos), 56 (3 photos), 63 (2 photos), 64 (left & right), 73
© **Debra Enzenbacher–Scott Polar Research Institute:** 32
(inset), 100
H. Armstrong Roberts: 10 (right); © **Profy,** 48
© **Dave G. Houser:** © **James C. Simmons,** 37, 43 (bottom
right)

© **Emilie Lepthien:** 73 (inset), 89 (bottom inset), 90 (inset)
NASA: 17 (left)
North Wind Picture Archives: 9 (left), 59 (right), 60 (2
photos), 61, 76
Photri: 18 (bottom), 68; © **Colin Monteath,** 17 (right), 20, 21
(left), 23, 25, 35 (right), 36, 43 (top right), 44 (top left &
bottom right), 46 (bottom), 89 (top inset), 94 (left), 98 (left),
99, 101; © **M. Fantin,** 18 (top)
Reuters/Bettmann: 99 (inset)
Root Resources: © **Mary & Lloyd McCarthy,** Cover Inset,
35 (left), 43 (bottom left), 96 (right), 97
© **Paul Sipiera:** 22, 75 (2 photos), 94 (top right), 95
Tom Stack & Associates: © **A. E. Zuckerman,** Cover, 46
(top left); © **Eye On The World Jack Stein Grove,** 39 (top);
© **Dave Watts,** 44 (top right), 90
Tony Stone Images: © **Terence Harding,** 102-103; © **Bryn
Campbell,** 121
SuperStock International, Inc.: © **Kurt Scholz,** 6, 42, 89;
© **Alan Briere,** 51 (top)
UPI/Bettmann: 59 (left), 64 (center), 66, 71, 78 (left), 81
(right), 82 (2 photos), 83 (right)
Valan: © **Johnny Johnson,** 5, 26, 39 (center & bottom), 40
(2 photos), 43 (top left), 46 (top right), 47; © **John Noble,**
21 (right), 32, 41 (right), 96 (left); © **Joyce Photographics,** 41
(left); © **Jeff Foott,** 48 (inset), 51 (bottom); © **Richard Sears,**
49, 50, 50 (inset)
Visuals Unlimited: © **Science VU,** 98 (right); © **Kjell B.
Sandved,** 4, © **Charles Preitner,** 11; © **Jeanette Thomas,** 24,
44 (center), 65, 94 (bottom right); © **Prance,** 44 (bottom left)
Tom Dunnington: Art on 111, 112
Len W. Meents: Maps and art on 12, 14, 15, 28, 65
**Courtesy Flag Research Center, Winchester,
Massachusetts 01890:** Flag on back cover
Cover: Iceberg and pack ice
Cover Inset: King penguins

A huge colony of adult and yearling king penguins

TABLE OF CONTENTS

Chapter 1   The Frozen Frontier. 7

Chapter 2   How Antarctica Formed. 13

Chapter 3   The Coldest Place on Earth. 27

Chapter 4   Plant and Animal Life. 34

Chapter 5   Early Days of Discovery. 52

Chapter 6   The Race to the South Pole: Triumph and Tragedy. 62

Chapter 7   Later Exploration. 72

Chapter 8   Cooperation Among Nations. 85

Chapter 9   Important Current and Future Issues. 93

Mini-Facts at a Glance. 106

Index. 122

The southern portion of the Transantarctic Mountains in Victoria Land meets the Ross Sea at Cape Hallett.

Chapter 1

THE FROZEN FRONTIER

Antarctica is the world's coldest, highest, driest, windiest, and fifth-largest continent. Ninety-eight percent of the continent is covered by ice. Its 5,100,000 square miles (13,209,000 square kilometers) cover nearly one-tenth of the earth's land surface. That makes it one-and-one-half times as large as the United States or twice the size of Australia. Yet it probably was not until 1820 that the first person ever set eyes upon this enormous continent.

TERRA AUSTRALIS INCOGNITA

That, however, did not keep people from thinking about Antarctica long before anyone had seen it. More than two thousand years ago the ancient Greeks already had figured out that the earth was round. One of these Greeks was the famous philosopher Aristotle. He felt that the southern hemisphere had to have a landmass large enough to balance the known lands in the northern hemisphere. He called this unseen land *Antarktikos,* and it soon began to appear on Greek maps. The word means "anti-Arctic" or the opposite of the Arctic.

The Greek philosopher Aristotle (left) thought there was a large landmass in the southern hemisphere and Ptolemy (right), the Egyptian astronomer, mathematician, and geographer, agreed.

In the second century A.D. an Egyptian geographer named Ptolemy accepted the Greek view that the earth was round and must have a southern continent. He felt that this *Terra Australis Incognita*, "unknown southern land," was populated and fertile. But there was a problem. Ptolemy believed that the land could not be reached by Europeans because it was cut off by a region of torrid heat and fire around the Equator. This equatorial region was simply too hot, Ptolemy believed, for anyone to pass through it. This idea took root and discouraged any southward exploration for twelve hundred years.

There was another, perhaps more important, reason why explorers did not sail south to test Ptolemy's ideas. Christian church leaders strongly discouraged it. They rejected the notion of a round earth and a populated southern continent because it raised too many troublesome questions. How, for example, could people separated by a barrier of impassable heat be descendants of Adam and Eve? How could they know about and be saved by

In the fifteenth century explorers such as Vasco da Gama (left) and Christopher Columbus (right) also believed the earth was round and had a southern continent and set out to prove it.

Christ's message? As a result of such beliefs, the study of geography and cartography experienced a significant setback. While ancient Greek maps showed a round earth with a southern continent, the maps of the Middle Ages showed a flat earth. Such maps pleased Christians because a flat earth, of course, could not have a southern hemisphere or a *Terra Australis Incognita*.

The Arabs, meanwhile, had preserved Ptolemy's teachings. Slowly, these ideas began to filter back into Europe. First the Moors, who were Arab Muslims, invaded and conquered most of southern Spain. Later the wars of the Crusades brought many Christian Europeans into contact with the Arab world. By the 1400s a new era of enlightenment, or *renaissance*, had dawned in Europe. The idea of a round earth and a southern continent was revived. With it came the great age of exploration. Now practical explorers, such as Vasco da Gama and Christopher Columbus, pushed farther south and west to see what the world was really like. Finally, in 1519, Ferdinand Magellan proved that the earth

After Magellan (left) proved the earth was round, Sir Francis Drake (center) and James Cook (right) began searching for Antarctica.

was a sphere by leading an expedition that was the first to circumnavigate the earth.

Everyone could see now that the Greeks had been right all along about the shape of the earth. Perhaps, people thought, the Greeks also were right about the great southern continent. Thus the search for Antarctica began. But despite the heroic efforts of men such as Francis Drake in 1577, Antonio de la Roche in 1675, Jean-Baptiste Charles Bouvet de Lozier in 1738, and James Cook in 1773, Antarctica itself remained a mystery. James Cook crossed the Antarctic Circle and circumnavigated Antarctica. In his journal he mentioned seeing large numbers of seals and whales in the waters. Whaling fleets from Europe and North America then set their sights southward to Antarctic waters.

Antarctica is like no other place on earth.

On January 27, 1820, a Russian explorer named Fabian von Bellingshausen was sailing inside the Antarctic Circle. Although he did not know it, he was just twenty miles (thirty-two kilometers) from the mainland of Antarctica. Suddenly, Bellingshausen spotted a huge wall of ice on the horizon. He wrote in his journal that he saw an "icefield covered with small hillrocks." Bellingshausen then noted his location and the weather. There was no celebration aboard his vessel, the *Vostok*. Bellingshausen did not realize that he had become the first person known to set eyes on the Antarctic continent. Perhaps, like many other explorers at the time, he expected to see exposed earth with some trees and signs of human habitation. But as we now know, Antarctica is like no other place on earth.

11

Chapter 2

HOW ANTARCTICA
FORMED

ISLAND CONTINENT

Antarctica is the most isolated continent in the world. South America, the nearest continent, is more than 600 miles (almost 1,000 kilometers) away. The coast of Australia is 1,550 miles (2,494 kilometers) north of Antarctica, and the southern tip of Africa is 2,500 miles (4,023 kilometers) away. Antarctica is separated by more than just distance. There is also a barrier of floating pack ice, masses of ice formed from seawater, that surrounds the continent. In addition, the seas are among the roughest in the world.

The continent of Antarctica is centered roughly on the geographic South Pole, the point where all the south latitudinal lines meet. (The magnetic South Pole is not the same place as the geographic South Pole. The South Magnetic Pole is the region where magnetic effects are the strongest. In other words, compass needles point to it.) Antarctica is both an island and a continent. It is considered an island because it is surrounded by water on all sides. The Indian Ocean, the Atlantic Ocean, and the Pacific Ocean all meet to form the stormy, ice-choked Antarctic (or Southern)

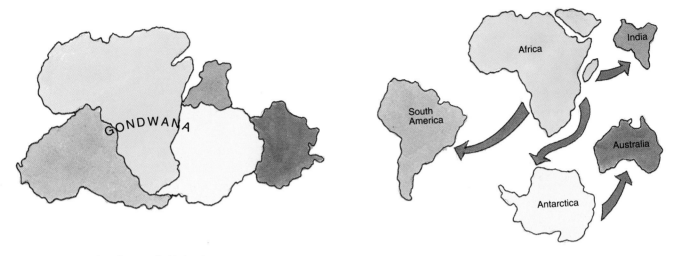

Gondwana (left) broke up and parts drifted away to form other continental landmasses (right).

Ocean that surrounds the landmass. Antarctica also is considered a continent because of its great size. It is nearly twice as large as the continent of Europe.

Many scientists believe that Antarctica was once part of a giant continent called Gondwana. They base this claim on fossils found in the late 1960s. These fossils are very similar to those found on other southern continents. At some point about 200 million years ago, these scientists believe, Gondwana broke up. As a result Antarctica drifted away from other continental landmasses. This continental drift was caused when plates in the earth's crust shifted.

Antarctica is a nearly perfectly round continent. Its circular shape is broken by the Antarctic Peninsula, the Weddell Sea, and the Ross Sea.

The continent is divided into two parts—East (Greater) Antarctica and West (Lesser) Antarctica—by the Transantarctic

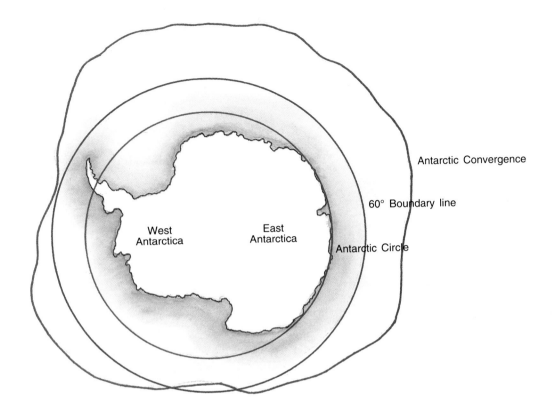

West
Antarctica

East
Antarctica

Antarctic Convergence

60° Boundary line

Antarctic Circle

Mountains. East Antarctica makes up the bulk of the continent's landmass. It is called *east* because it is mainly in the eastern longitudes. West Antarctica, located primarily in the western longitudes, is really a group of islands tied together by permanent ice.

ANTARCTIC TERMS AND PLACE NAMES

The Antarctic region includes everything inside the Antarctic climatic zone. It extends northward from the South Pole (90 degrees south) across the Antarctic Circle, at 66 degrees 32 minutes south, to where the cold polar waters meet the subtropical waters of the Atlantic, Pacific, and Indian Oceans. The meeting of these waters forms an irregular biological boundary called the Antarctic Convergence. Along this boundary, which is approximately twenty-five miles (forty kilometers) wide, there is a sharp drop in surface water temperatures of 5 degrees Fahrenheit (2.8 degrees Celsius). South of the Convergence the Southern Ocean maintains a relatively constant temperature of 28 degrees Fahrenheit (minus 2.2 degrees Celsius). In general the Antarctic Convergence occurs between 50 degrees and 60 degrees south latitude.

The Antarctic Treaty of 1959 described the area in Antarctica over which its terms apply, namely the area south of 60 degrees south latitude. This treaty was signed by the twelve nations that were actively involved in conducting scientific research in the region during the International Geophysical Year (IGY) of 1957-1958. Current maps of the continent of Antarctica include the mainland and all the permanent ice shelves that are attached to it.

Places in Antarctica are often named in honor of an explorer's monarch or members of royal families. For example, East Antarctica has Victoria Land, Queen Maud Land, and the Prince Charles Mountains. Many other places are named after the explorers who first traveled there. West Antarctica has Palmer Land (after Nathaniel Palmer, the nineteenth-century U. S. explorer), the Ross Ice Shelf (after the English explorer Sir James Clark Ross), and the Bellingshausen Sea (after the Russian explorer Admiral Fabian Bellingshausen).

THE ICE COVER

When you think of Antarctica, think of ice, hundreds of billions of tons of ice. More than 90 percent of the earth's permanent ice is found in Antarctica. Astronauts, looking down from space, have said that the Antarctic ice sheet "radiates light like a great white

Left: A photo taken in 1972 by the Apollo 17 *crew as they traveled to the moon shows the continent of Africa in the center and the white continent of Antarctica at the bottom.*
Right: Nunataks, *or mountain peaks, appear through the ice.*

lantern across the bottom of the earth." This awesome ice sheet is the earth's largest storehouse of freshwater, built over countless years by falling snow that did not melt. It contains approximately 68 percent of the earth's freshwater, some 7.2 million cubic miles (30 million cubic kilometers).

In many places the ice is 2 miles (3 kilometers or about 3,000 meters) thick. Almost all the land is under ice. In a few places, however, mountain peaks appear through the ice; such features are called *nunataks*. There are also a few coastal areas that are ice free. These comprise less than 2 percent of the continent.

The tremendous accumulation of ice makes Antarctica by far the *highest* continent on the earth, with an average elevation of 7,500 feet (2,286 meters). The second-highest continent is Asia, with an average elevation of 3,000 feet (914 meters). In another sense, however, the ice makes Antarctica the *lowest* continent on

Above: Part of the Ross Ice Shelf
Below: An aerial view of an iceberg that broke away from the Ross Ice Shelf.

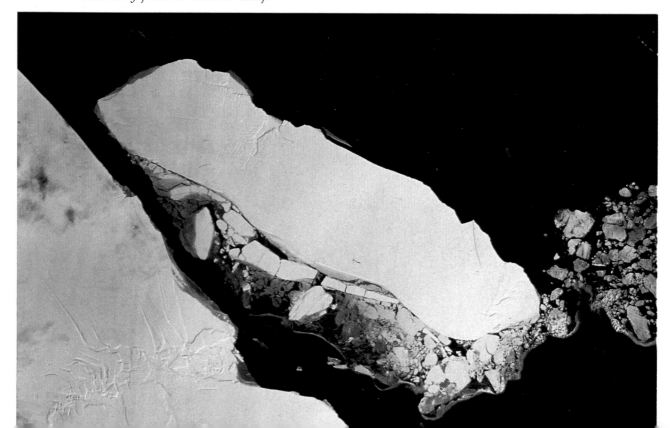

earth. The weight of the ice pack is so great that the bedrock beneath is pushed downward. In many places the landmass is well below sea level. If all the ice melted, this massive burden would be released. Scientists estimate that the bedrock would then rise some 2,000 feet (610 meters).

ICE SHELVES, GLACIERS, AND ICEBERGS

The ice found in Antarctica takes several forms. The most prominent is the ice sheet that covers most of the continent. In addition, there are ice shelves, glaciers, and icebergs.

Ice shelves, floating slabs of ice jutting out from the land, rise and fall with the ocean tide. They form the boundaries between the ice sheet and the ice front where the sheet disintegrates into icebergs. These ice shelves roughly double the size of Antarctica in the winter. The inner boundary of an ice shelf is defined as the place where the ice sheet or glacier begins to float. The outer boundary, the ice front, is where the ice shelf begins to break up to form icebergs. The largest ice shelf in Antarctica is the Ross Ice Shelf. It is four times the size of New York State and almost as large as Texas. The Ross Ice Shelf, next to the ice sheet, is approximately 3,000 feet (914 meters) thick. From there it slopes down to a height of 650 feet (198 meters) where it meets the Ross Sea. The Ross Ice Shelf is constantly fed by glaciers, such as the Beardmore, Nimrod, and Byrd. Other large ice shelves in Antarctica include the Amery, Ronne, and Filchner.

Glaciers are created over hundreds of years by densely packed snow. When the weight of a glacier becomes great enough, it begins to move through mountain valleys. A glacier moves because of friction created by the pressure of the ice on the

Floating pack ice and icebergs in Hope Bay near the Antarctic Peninsula

bedrock. Friction creates heat and melts a little of the ice. The friction of the ice moving across the rocks also creates heat. This thin film of water provides the lubricant to set the glacier in motion. Most glaciers do not move very rapidly. The fastest-moving glacier in Antarctica is the Shirase in eastern Queen Maud Land. It moves approximately 1.2 miles (2 kilometers) per year.

Glaciers vary greatly in size. They can be as small as a couple of miles long and 500 feet (152 meters) wide. The largest glacier on the earth is in East Antarctica; the Lambert Glacier is 25 miles (40 kilometers) wide and more than 248 miles (400 kilometers) long. It flows through the Prince Charles Mountains. All glaciers serve the same function. They drain the interior of ice and snow.

Icebergs are created when huge chunks of an ice shelf, an ice cliff, or a glacier break off. The process is called *calving.* About 80 percent of all icebergs are calved from ice shelves. These are often

Icebergs often take on fantastic shapes as they disintegrate.

unbelievably huge. One iceberg sighted in 1956 measured 208 miles (335 kilometers) by 60 miles (97 kilometers), exceeding the size of some small countries. Smaller icebergs calve off ice cliffs and glaciers.

Although there is ice flow from the continent and further ice is lost by the calving of icebergs, new ice is added by snowfall.

Antarctic icebergs typically drift northward. As they age and melt they usually break up into smaller icebergs. They also become less angular and more rounded. Only 10 to 15 percent of an iceberg normally appears above the water's surface. If they are not trapped in a bay or inlet, most icebergs eventually reach the Antarctic Convergence. This is usually as far as they travel unless an intense storm carries them farther north. The ocean currents then sweep them from west to east until they melt. An average iceberg normally lasts several years before melting.

A valley glacier in the Transantarctic Mountains

MOUNTAINS AND DRY VALLEYS

Although only about 2 percent of the land is exposed, we know that Antarctica is a very mountainous continent. Scientists have learned the shape of the snow-covered land surface by using radio-echo soundings to penetrate the ice. The Transantarctic Mountains are the longest range on the continent, stretching 3,000 miles (4,828 kilometers) from the Ross Sea to the Weddell Sea. Several mountain peaks exceed 14,000 feet (4,267 meters). The highest mountain in Antarctica is the Vinson Massif at 16,859 feet (5,140 meters) in the Sentinel Range of the Ellsworth Mountains.

The Wright Valley, Taylor Valley, and Victoria Valley are the largest continuous areas of ice-free land on the continent. They are known as the dry valleys. These dry valleys rank among the most

Wright Valley, a dry valley in Victoria Land

incredible sights on earth. No other place on our planet so closely compares to the landscape of Mars. Each valley is approximately twenty-five miles (forty kilometers) long and three miles (five kilometers) wide.

What makes these valleys so remarkable is their dryness. No rain is known to have fallen in these valleys for more than two million years. Falling snow evaporates long before it reaches the ground. The air is so dry that nothing decomposes. One very strange sight is the presence of Weddell seal carcasses scattered throughout these dry valleys. This suggests that at one time the ocean was closer to the valleys than it is today. These valleys might also have been underwater. The extreme dryness of the area has preserved the seals' dead carcasses like the mummies of ancient Egypt. Some of the carcasses are more than one thousand years old. Little has changed in these valleys except for the erosion caused by ceaseless winds.

Mt. Erebus, the largest volcano on Ross Island, is still active.

ISLANDS AND VOLCANOES

Antarctica has a number of important islands. The Antarctic coastal islands, which include Alexander, Roosevelt, and Ross Islands, are more or less covered with ice most of the year. These islands are attached to the mainland by ice for nine months each year. The cold temperatures prevent rain on these islands, but snow does occur. The weather is similar to that found on the nearby mainland. Ross Island is the home of four volcanoes. Mount Erebus, at 12,444 feet (3,793 meters), is the largest of these and is still active.

Scientists from the United States National Aeronautics and Space Administration (NASA) have begun to use robots to explore inside the volcano. They hope to measure temperatures close to the molten lava lake at the crater's bottom. They also hope to show how robotics might be used to explore the moon as well as Mars.

The Antarctic maritime islands are farther out to sea and are surrounded by pack ice during the winter. They include the South Orkney, South Shetland, and Balleny Islands. Several of these

Southern elephant seal pups and king penguins and their brown chicks on South Georgia, a subantarctic island

islands are home to a number of penguins and various species of seabirds such as petrels, terns, and skuas.

Still farther out to sea are the subantarctic islands. The most well known of these are South Georgia, Heard Island, and MacDonald Island. These islands lie near the Antarctic Convergence between 48 degrees and 60 degrees south latitude. South Georgia was an important nineteenth-century base for seal hunters. From 1904 to 1966 it was the largest whaling station in the area. The island is no longer used for such purposes.

These windy, cold, and wet subantarctic islands are rarely blocked by pack ice, although 90 percent of Heard Island is covered by glacial ice. Tussock grass grows on these islands, and they are also the summer breeding home for many elephant and fur seals. Still, they have considerably hostile environments with fierce winds that often sweep across the ice caps and glaciers that form there.

Chapter 3

THE COLDEST PLACE
ON EARTH

There is a reason why the first explorers did not find any native people, land animals, or trees in Antarctica. The environment is simply too cold and inhospitable. Just how bitterly cold it can be may be difficult for people who live in temperate regions to imagine. For example, the coldest winter day in the southern United States such as North Carolina or Alabama would be considered a delightful day by Antarctic standards.

Even people who live in the northern United States may find it difficult to imagine just how cold it gets in Antarctica. For example, the lowest temperature ever recorded in the state of Vermont was minus 50 degrees Fahrenheit (minus 45.6 degrees Celsius) in December 1933. The lowest temperature ever recorded in Antarctica was minus 129.3 degrees Fahrenheit (minus 89.6 degrees Celsius) at Vostok Station on July 2, 1983; a difference of nearly 80 degrees Fahrenheit. This does not even take into account the wind-chill factor (the combination of wind and temperature). It gets breezy in Vermont every once in a while, but the relentless winds of Antarctica are almost always blowing, especially along

Opposite page: Paradise Harbor near the Antarctic Peninsula

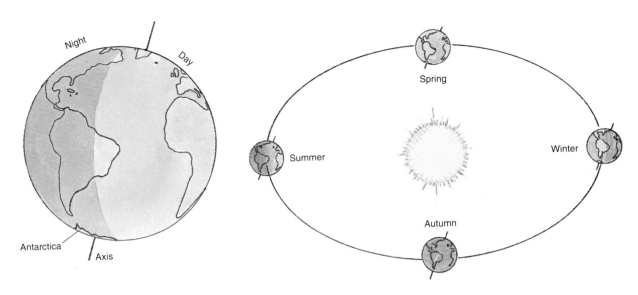

The earth tilts on its axis as it rotates around the sun.
This affects the angle at which the sun hits Antarctica.

the coast. People who work in Antarctica need to be very careful, especially during outdoor activity. If the wind-chill factor drops low enough, any exposed human flesh may freeze, a condition known as *frostbite.*

WHY IS IT SO COLD?

Some people might compare the Antarctic with the Arctic. Is the northern polar region as cold as the southern polar region? The answer, in a word, is no. The mean temperatures in the Arctic are approximately twenty degrees Fahrenheit (eleven degrees Celsius) warmer than they are at a similar latitude in the Antarctic.

To be sure, both polar regions are very cold most of the time. This is due mainly to the way the earth tilts on its axis as it rotates around the sun. The 23.5-degree axial tilt results in long winter nights and long summer days in both polar regions.

The tilt also affects the angle at which the sun's radiation hits the earth. In the tropics, near the Equator, the sun is directly overhead and its radiation produces great heat. In the polar regions, however, the sun–even on the first day of summer–is low in the sky. This means that the sunlight strikes the polar regions at a much more oblique, or indirect, angle. As a result, the sun's radiation generates a great deal less heat. So, despite the fact that the polar regions receive as much *annual* daylight as do the tropical regions, they receive much less solar radiation.

Why, then, is there such a difference between the Arctic and the Antarctic? The basic reason has to do with geography. The Arctic region is essentially an ocean surrounded by continents. Antarctica, on the other hand, is a vast continent surrounded by oceans. The Arctic Ocean is a source of stored heat that helps to modify the climate of the Arctic region. Ice-free water in the Arctic reflects only about 5 percent of the sun's radiation. By contrast, in the Antarctic the immense continental ice cap intensifies the harsh polar climate, because snow reflects more than 80 percent of the sun's radiation.

Antarctica also plays an important role in the world's weather patterns. The South Pole, like the North Pole, draws warmer air toward it. But the cold high winds found near the poles drive the warm air back. This process, not fully understood, creates great low pressure systems, or storms. That is why the seas around Antarctica are almost always stormy. In the nineteenth century sailors nicknamed the southern latitudes the "Roaring Forties" and the "Furious Fifties."

A BALANCING ACT

For most of the year the continental ice cap loses more heat than it gains from the sun. Why, then, doesn't Antarctica grow colder and colder? There must be another source of heat besides solar energy. The answer is found in the three layers of the atmosphere above the continent. The first and third are cold air layers. They move cold air away from the continent. The middle layer, however, is warmer. The moist air in this layer travels from the more temperate regions over the oceans. As this air approaches the South Pole, it gives off energy in the form of heat, as it condenses and freezes. In this way, Antarctica's climate remains balanced and stable.

TEMPERATURES

Temperatures in Antarctica vary greatly from place to place. In general, however, they range from cold to colder to coldest. The coastal regions are generally warmer than the interior. The Antarctic Peninsula, the warmest part of the continent, can get quite warm during the summer months. Once in a while the temperature climbs as high as 50 degrees Fahrenheit (10 degrees Celsius), but elsewhere the temperatures are much colder.

Mean summer temperatures along most of the coast average thirty-two degrees Fahrenheit (zero degrees Celsius). In the interior mean summer temperatures range between minus four degrees and minus thirty-one degrees Fahrenheit (minus twenty degrees and minus thirty-five degrees Celsius). During the dark winter months, temperatures drop sharply. Along the coast the warmest temperature one can expect is somewhere between minus four degrees and minus twenty-two degrees Fahrenheit (minus twenty degrees and minus thirty degrees Celsius). In the interior the bleak sunless winter days rarely get much warmer than minus forty degrees Fahrenheit (minus forty degrees Celsius) and often get as cold as minus ninety-four degrees Fahrenheit (minus seventy degrees Celsius).

STRONG WINDS

As incredible as Antarctica's cold is, its winds are equally impressive. Antarctica is not only the coldest continent on the earth, it is also the windiest. *Katabatic* winds are caused by cold air racing over the high ice cap, then flowing down to the low coastal regions.

Katabatic winds can be extremely strong. They have made Commonwealth Bay on George V Coast the windiest place on earth. Winds there often blow between 50 miles (80 kilometers) and 90 miles (145 kilometers) an hour for several days in a row. Winds reach much higher speeds during storms. During blizzards, gusts of more than 120 miles (193 kilometers) an hour are quite common.

BLIZZARDS

Blizzards are another brutal fact of life for anyone trying to work in Antarctica. Usually when we think of blizzards we think of a snowstorm with high winds, but nature has its own set of rules for Antarctica. Although snowfall occurs, falling snow is not

High winds create blizzards and whip up sastrugi *(inset), irregularly shaped ridges of snow.*

needed because powerful winds simply blow snow that is already on the ground. The sky can be perfectly clear overhead, while on the ground the wind is whipping the snow around. Wind whips the snow into irregular shapes called *sastrugi,* and it is very difficult to walk on their uneven surface. Outdoor work is impossible. A blizzard might last several days. Blizzards strike some areas more often than others. On average, however, there are between eight and ten major blizzards a year. During these times whiteout conditions exist, when it is impossible to distinguish the horizon in the distance or to see your hand in front of your face. Many explorers and field parties have been lost during these conditions. It's no wonder that one explorer named an Antarctic research site, "The Home of the Blizzard."

PRECIPITATION

Despite all of its stored-up snow and ice, Antarctica is the driest continent on the earth. On the polar ice cap, annual snowfall is only 1 to 2 inches (2.5 to 5 centimeters). That is why it is often called the White Desert. More precipitation falls along the coast and in the coastal mountains where it may average 10 to 20 inches (25 to 51 centimeters) per year. One place in Antarctica that occasionally gets warm enough for a little rain or drizzle to fall is the northern tip of the Antarctic Peninsula.

CYCLONES

Great ocean storms, called cyclones, constantly rage from west to east around the Antarctic continent. Naturally, that makes the Southern Ocean the stormiest sea to be found anywhere on the earth. These cyclones are caused when warm, moist ocean air strikes the cold, dry polar air. Cyclones develop between 60 degrees and 65 degrees south latitude. Gradually they swirl toward the coast of Antarctica and usually lose their force well before they reach land. Still, they play a vital role in the exchange of heat and moisture between the tropics and the cold polar air of Antarctica.

Chapter 4

PLANT AND ANIMAL LIFE

We have already seen how the two polar regions differ in terms of geography and climate. They also differ greatly with respect to plant and animal life. The Arctic region teems with life, but much of the Antarctic region appears nearly or totally barren because most of the Antarctic continent is too cold and too dry to support anything but a few specially adapted species of plants and animals. So a visitor hoping to see poppies, buttercups, reindeer, caribou, or polar bears needs to visit the Arctic, because these species do not occur in the Antarctic.

That, however, does not mean that there is *no* life in the Antarctic. Far from it. The flora and fauna of the Antarctic may not be as diverse as they are in the Arctic, but they are often prolific. One just has to look in the right places, sometimes through a microscope!

PLANT LIFE

The pearlwort *(Colobanthus quitensis)* and grass *(Deschampsia antarctica)* are the only two flowering plants that grow south of 60

The most common large plants are mosses and lichens. Lichens grow in colors from gray and black to yellowish-orange.

degrees south latitude. Both exist only in a small area on or near the Antarctic Peninsula. In the Arctic, on the other hand, there are nearly one hundred different types of flowering plants that survive at 84 degrees north latitude.

The most common large plants found in Antarctica are mosses and lichens, plants that are a combination of algae and fungi. They are found along the coast of the continent as well as on the Antarctic Peninsula. Green, nonflowering plants called *liverworts* are found along the warmer western side of the Antarctic Peninsula (although only one liverwort, *Cephalozrilla exiliflora,* has actually been found on the continent). On the microscopic level

Green and red algae color the snow on the Antarctic Peninsula.

life exists in the form of bacteria, algae, and fungi. Brightly colored snow algae often form beautiful red, yellow, or green patches on glaciers and ice caps.

LAND ANIMALS

The land animals of Antarctica are small, ranging from protozoans (microscopic single-cell creatures) to insects about one-half inch (twelve millimeters) long. In other words, beyond a few mites and midges, there are no other land animals native to the area. In contrast, life in the sea and along the coast of Antarctica and its islands is often abundant.

OCEAN ANIMALS AND THE FOOD CHAIN

The land is too cold and too barren to support much life, but the sea is not. A wide variety of animals live in or on the water surrounding Antarctica. These range from small floating animals called *zooplankton* to birds and large mammals. There are also many fish species in the Antarctic. These fish have adapted to their frigid environment by producing a kind of antifreeze. This

Krill are the most abundant zooplankton in the Antarctic.

substance prevents ice crystals from forming in their bodies. Some Antarctic fish also have no red blood cells, which gives them an eerie, creamy-white color.

The Antarctic food chain is highly evolved. It begins with small floating plants called *phytoplankton*. These plants feed on the rich nutrients found in coastal waters. The zooplankton then feed on the phytoplankton. The zooplankton, in turn, become an important source of food for many fish, birds, and mammals. As elsewhere, the larger animals also feed on others that are smaller. Whales, for example, will eat fish, squid, and krill. Leopard seals may eat penguins.

THE ANTARCTIC KRILL

Antarctic krill, tiny shrimplike creatures that measure, on average, about 1.5 inches (3.8 centimeters), are the most abundant zooplankton in the Antarctic. Krill are essential to almost every other form of life in the Antarctic because they provide the main source of food for many fish, seabirds, penguins, seals, and whales. The icy waters surrounding Antarctica are brimming with Antarctic krill. They can be seen during the day as large red patches on the ocean. At night they shimmer and glow like billions of fireflies beneath the sea.

PENGUINS

The absence of any land predators and the presence of a rich offshore food supply make the Antarctic an ideal environment for many species of birds. The most famous and beloved of these birds is the penguin. Scientists believe that these delightful creatures evolved around forty to fifty million years ago. Today millions of penguins make their home in the Antarctic region.

Penguins have oily feathers that provide a waterproof coat and a thick layer of fat for insulation. Although most birds have hollow bones to make flying easier, the bones of the flightless penguin are solid. This adds weight and makes it easier for them to dive deep into the water to feed. Penguins often amuse visitors because of the way they waddle awkwardly on land or toboggan over the snow on their bellies with their wings outstretched. In the water, however, they are superb swimmers.

Although there are eighteen known living species of penguins, only seven of them are found in the Antarctic. Each species differs from the others in one or more ways such as coloring, size, weight, feeding habits, and breeding cycle. The four species considered "southern" penguins, because they live on or near the coast of Antarctica, are Adélie, emperor, chinstrap, and gentoo penguins. Of these four the Adélie and emperor are considered "true" Antarctic penguins because they live on continental Antarctica. The other three are the macaroni, rockhopper, and king.

The chinstrap earned its name from the distinctive black line beneath its chin. Chinstraps are found on Antarctic maritime islands and along the western shore of the Antarctic Peninsula. Gentoo penguins breed mainly on subantarctic islands, with most living on South Georgia. Their total population numbers only about 350,000.

Above: Millions of the noisy and often aggressive chinstrap penguins live on the South Orkney, South Shetland, and South Sandwich Islands.   Right: A gentoo penguin with a young chick   Below: Gentoo penguins breed mainly on subantarctic islands.

King penguins (left) are easily recognized by the orange "collar" around their neck and the side of their heads. Macaroni penguins (right) have bright orange-yellow plumes originating from the center of their heads.

The three species considered "northern" penguins, because they breed on the subantarctic islands, are king, macaroni, and rockhopper penguins. There are millions of macaroni penguins on Heard Island and South Georgia. The rockhopper is the smallest of all the Antarctic penguins. This aggressive bird is easily recognized because it has long silklike golden tassels above its eyes. Rockhoppers breed mostly on cliffs or slopes of islands near the Antarctic Convergence.

Of all the penguins the Adélie is the most plentiful and can be found over the widest area. Adélies spend their winters on the pack ice away from the Antarctic continent. In October they return to land to nest in large rookeries, or colonies, often located along the rocky coast of Antarctica. The males arrive first to occupy available nest spaces. The females arrive a few days later and courting begins. In November the female usually lays two

*An Adélie penguin with her chick (above) and
a rockhopper incubating an egg (right)*

eggs, then returns to the sea to feed, while the male incubates the eggs in the nest. After seven to ten days the female returns to help the male. It takes a little more than a month for the chicks to hatch.

The emperor penguin is the largest of all penguins. Although it is the only Antarctic bird never to set foot on land, the emperor breeds on sea ice attached to the mainland. Unlike other penguins, emperors hatch their eggs during the coldest months of the Antarctic winter. The female lays one egg in May or early June. The male then takes over the care and protection of the egg. While the mother goes off to feed in the ocean, the father balances the egg on his feet and then keeps it warm by covering it with a special fold of skin called a brood patch. There he stays for nearly two months, weathering bitterly cold temperatures and howling blizzards, until the egg hatches. During this time, the

By the time an emperor chick is six weeks old, both of its parents must find food for its ravenous appetite.

fasting male will lose 40 percent of his body weight. Emperor penguins often huddle together to stay warm, especially during the long winter months. Most chicks hatch as the females return from the sea. The mother then cares for the chick while the father goes to the sea to feed.

OTHER ANTARCTIC BIRDS

Antarctica is home to a wide variety of seabirds that are well adapted to the harsh climate of the southern polar region. Their dense plumage and body fat protect them from the cold. These birds are equipped to grab food from the surface of the sea. Antarctic seabirds breed along the coast. Twenty-four species of

Other birds living in the Antarctic include (clockwise from top left) the brown skua, the wandering albatross, the blue-eyed cormorant, and the giant petrel.

petrels can be found south of the Antarctic Convergence, including the wandering albatross, the southern giant fulmar, the dove prion, and the snow petrel.

An additional twelve species of shore and land birds also are found south of the Antarctic Convergence. They feed in the shallow waters near the shore or on land. Among the shorebirds are the blue-eyed cormorant, the Dominican gull, the Antarctic tern, and the brown skua. The skua, with its hooked bill and sharp claws, is a determined scavenger, who often takes penguin eggs and attacks weak penguin chicks. Land birds feed exclusively ashore. These birds are also scavengers. Land birds include the wattled sheathbill, the South Georgia pintail, and the South Georgia pipit.

Top left and right: Weddell seals can stay underwater for up to an hour at a time.   Right: Ross seals are the smallest of the Antarctic seals.   Bottom left and right: Leopard seals are fierce predators and can travel fast because of their slender bodies.

TRUE SEALS AND THE FUR SEAL

There are six different species of seals that live in the Antarctic. Five of these seals—the Weddell, Ross, leopard, crabeater, and elephant—are considered true or "earless" seals. True seals have no external ear, although their hearing is quite good on land and in the water. Ashore these seals move rather awkwardly, using their short flippers. In the water they are good swimmers. The southern fur seal has a visible ear. It also has longer flippers than the true seal, which makes it very agile on land as well as in the water. Seals have blubber and dense fur to insulate them from the cold.

The remarkable Weddell seals live and breed farther south than any other seal. During the winter months they can survive under the permanent ice attached to the continent. Because they are mammals and not fish, they need to come up for air. They get the oxygen they need by using their sawlike teeth to cut holes in the ice. Still, Weddell seals can stay underwater for up to an hour at a time, and have been known to dive 2,000 feet (610 meters) or more to catch fish. They use sonar to locate food.

Ross seals live mostly on the thickest areas of pack ice and are the least plentiful. This makes them hard to find and study. As a result Ross seals are the least well known of all the Antarctic seals. They are also the smallest of the Antarctic seals.

Leopard seals are fierce predators. They live on northern edges of pack ice. Leopard seals can often be found in the sea near penguin rookeries, where they leap up and capture unwary prey. Females are 10 percent larger than males.

Crabeater seals are the most numerous large seal on the earth. At present, it is estimated that there are more than 40 million

Crabeater seals (top left) spend most of their time in the water and do not come to land often. Elephant seals (top right) usually return to the same place each year in the fall to breed. An elephant seal bull (above) playing with a young pup.

Because fur seals can bend their hind limbs, they get around easily on land. Their pups have black fur.

within the Antarctic region. They live on pack ice. Females are slightly larger than the males.

Elephant seals are the largest of all seals. They get their name from their *proboscis,* or trunk, which they can inflate to scare off other males or attract females. They live on subantarctic islands and eat squid and fish. Elephant seals were almost wiped out by hunters who sought their oil. They now are protected under international law, along with Ross, crabeater, leopard, and Weddell seals. Unlike most seals, the males are much larger than the females.

The fur of the southern fur seal has two layers, a dense velvety inner layer, which is waterproof, and an outer layer of coarse hair. Merciless hunting forced the southern fur seal to the brink of extinction during previous centuries. The hunters, called sealers, wanted the skins of the seal. Common sense prevailed, however, and international laws were passed to protect Antarctic seals. Today fur seals are making a comeback. They feed on krill, fish, and squid. Male fur seals are larger than females.

The humpback whale arches backward as it leaps out of the water.
Baleen (inset) in a whale's mouth serves as a filtering system for food.

WHALES

Whales, which travel the oceans of the earth, also are found in the Antarctic. Among those that make their home in Antarctic waters for at least part of the year are blue, fin, sei, minke, humpback, and southern right whales. These mammals make up the group called *southern baleen whales.* The chief characteristic of these whales is a bristly substance called *baleen* located in plates in the mouth that serve as a filtering system to strain food such as krill from the water. The other type of whale is the toothed whale. The two most important toothed whales found in the Antarctic are the sperm whale and the orca, or killer, whale. All baleen and toothed whales are now protected by international

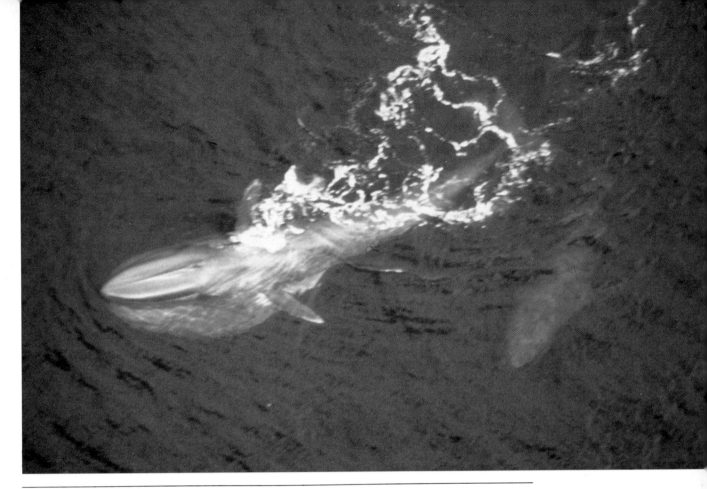

A mother blue whale and her offspring are members of an endangered species.

agreements in an attempt to reverse the damage caused by excessive hunting in the past.

The blue whale is thought to be the biggest creature that has ever lived on the earth. The largest one known measured 124 feet (37.8 meters) and weighed 180 tons (more than 163,000 kilograms). Scientists believe that before the days of whaling, blue whales numbered around 200,000. Today there may be as few as 1,000 left. Whether these magnificent creatures will survive in the long run is uncertain. Fin, sei, and minke whales closely resemble the blue whale. The humpback whale looks different from the others because it has a less streamlined body and much longer flippers.

The sperm whale uses echo sounding to find its prey and can dive (inset) to a depth of more than 3,000 feet (more than 1,000 meters).

The sperm whale is the largest of the toothed whales, measuring up to 60 feet (18 meters) and weighing as much as 70 tons (63,500 kilograms). The sperm whale, by far the best diving whale, can dive 3,300 feet (1,006 meters). Only the males are known to migrate to Antarctic waters. The orca, or killer whale, more closely resembles dolphins than other whales. One of the most intelligent of marine animals, orcas are also the earth's largest carnivore. They hunt in packs along the edge of the ice to feed on squid, aquatic birds, seals, and penguins.

Above: The orca whale, which resembles a dolphin, is the world's largest carnivore.   Below: An orca attacks an elephant seal.

Chapter 5

EARLY DAYS OF DISCOVERY

In Chapter 1 Fabian von Bellingshausen, the Russian explorer, was named as the first person to sight Antarctica, on January 27, 1820. Many people agree with this, but some dispute the claim. Some maintain that Edward Bransfield, an English explorer, was the first to sight the continent on January 30, 1820. Some argue that it was really Nathaniel Palmer, a U. S. sealer, who first spotted the mainland on November 18, 1820. Historical accuracy and national pride, of course, play a role here. In the end, however, the most important outcome was that the great southern continent was finally found. The exploration of Antarctica was about to begin.

JOHN DAVIS

During the early 1800s, the murderous hunt for the southern fur seal carried ships farther and farther south. As soon as the seals in one place were wiped out, the sealers looked for new hunting

Nathaniel Palmer (left) sighted the mainland of Antarctica in 1820. An 1871 drawing (right) of seal hunting

grounds. So it should come as no great surprise that the first person to set foot on Antarctica was a sealer, not an explorer. He was a little-known U. S. sealer from Connecticut named John Davis.

In January 1821, Captain Davis of the *Cecilia* arrived at the South Shetland Islands, southeast of the tip of South America, looking for seals. Several other sealers had already begun their work and made it clear "with guns, pistols & swords" that they did not want any competition. On January 30, Davis decided that it was best to move farther south to find new territory. After stopping at Smith and Low Islands, he headed farther south. On February 7, he wrote in the ship's log, discovered in 1952, that he saw "a Large bay, the Land high and covered entirely with snow. . . . I think this Southern Land to be a Continent." Davis then landed a boat in the vicinity of Cape Charles. He later returned to Connecticut, and little else is known about his life.

JAMES WEDDELL

One Englishman, James Weddell, had both a sea and a seal named after him. Weddell was a sealer, but he also had the heart and determination of an explorer. In 1822, he took two ships, the *Jane* and the *Beaufoy*, on a sealing expedition. If no seals could be found, he planned to explore beyond points reached by any previous explorers.

On January 13, 1823, Weddell landed in the South Orkneys just northeast of the Antarctic Peninsula. There he found fur seals along with several unknown species of seals, one of which became known as the Weddell seal. His search for fur seals elsewhere proved disappointing. At this point the sealer turned explorer. On February 4 he ordered his two ships to head south. Blessed by unusually warm weather and relatively ice-free water, he sailed farther south than any other explorer. Finally, on February 20, 1823, he reached 74 degrees south latitude. He decided at that point to turn back because the season would soon change. The vast sea he had entered became known as the Weddell Sea. It was not until 1911 that another ship returned to this area.

THREE NATIONAL EXPEDITIONS

During 1840 and 1841 France, the United States, and Great Britain sent major expeditions to Antarctica. Each had scientific and political goals. The first to arrive were the French under the command of the scholarly Jules-Sébastien-César Dumont d'Urville. By January 19, 1840, d'Urville's ships, the *Astrolabe* and the *Zélée*, had crossed the Antarctic Circle, and the men sighted an icebound coastline that stretched as far as the eye could see. They had sighted the Antarctic continent. The ships, making their way through ice-clogged waters, followed the coast to the west. The icebergs were so close and massive that the commands shouted on board echoed off the ice. On January 21, several men went ashore and claimed the land for France. Captain d'Urville named his discovery *Terre Adélie,* "Adélie's Land," after his wife. Adélie penguins also were named by d'Urville's expedition.

Up to this point the French had enjoyed relatively mild weather, but then a violent storm struck and both ships were badly damaged. On January 29, just as d'Urville was ready to turn back, a ship flying the United States flag suddenly appeared through the fog. It was the *Porpoise,* part of the United States Exploring Expedition under the command of Charles Wilkes. Just as suddenly, for reasons that remain unclear, the *Porpoise* turned and disappeared. There were no greetings shouted, nor were any signals exchanged.

The Wilkes expedition has often been described as the most ill-prepared and controversial in U.S. history. From the beginning the expedition was plagued by personal feuds and political corruption. The ships were not in good condition, the equipment was poor, and the budget was inadequate. Even the selection of the forty-year-old Wilkes over older, higher-ranking officers caused bitter dispute.

Yet if it had not been for the forceful Wilkes, the whole enterprise might have collapsed. As it was, things turned out badly enough. The ships leaked. The men suffered from disease, exposure, malnutrition, and exhaustion. Several times Wilkes pushed them to the verge of mutiny, but somehow he remained in control. In the end the U.S. expedition achieved one of the

Although the expedition was badly planned, Charles Wilkes (left inset) somehow succeeded in exploring the coastline of East Antarctica. The ships under the command of James Clark Ross (right inset), the Erebus *and* Terror, *were trapped in pack ice.*

great feats of exploration. They explored 1,240 miles (1,996 kilometers) of East Antarctica's coastline, a large section of which now bears their captain's name–Wilkes Land.

In contrast, the expedition of England's James Clark Ross was as carefully planned as Wilkes' was poorly planned. The two ships used by Ross, the *Erebus* and the *Terror,* were stoutly built and specially outfitted for the Antarctic. Each had its own surgeon to treat those who were sick or injured. Ross brought enough food to last three years. He carried tins of preserved meats, soups, and vegetables. He also brought along cranberries, pickled cabbage, and pepper. In addition, Ross took the latest equipment for polar exploring, such as strong canvas, ice saws, and a portable forge. Ross even handpicked his own crew.

As it turned out, Ross needed these strong ships. On January 7, 1841, the *Erebus* and the *Terror* were trapped in pack ice. A fierce storm then hit the two helpless ships. Massive waves and huge blocks of ice battered the vessels. Ross later wrote, "Each of us could only secure a hold, waiting the issue with resignation to the will of Him who alone could bring us through such extreme danger."

Somehow the ships and their crews survived. The storm had a silver lining—it broke up the pack ice. Within a couple of days, the ships again set sail. Ross sailed into the Ross Sea and discovered the Admiralty Mountains and Victoria Land. On January 28, 1841, Ross saw one of Antarctica's few active volcanoes and named it Mount Erebus, after his ship. He named a nearby inactive volcano Mount Terror. The men continued sailing when suddenly they spotted a truly awesome sight. Ross saw a low white line reaching as far as the eye could see and wrote: "It presented an extraordinary appearance, gradually increasing in height, as we got nearer to it, and proving at length to be a perpendicular cliff of ice, between 150 and 200 feet [46 and 61 meters] above the level of the sea, perfectly flat and level at the top."

For several weeks Ross sailed along this great ice barrier, known today as the Ross Ice Shelf. He could find no breaks or openings in it. It just grew higher and higher. Ross wrote, "We might with equal chance of success try to sail through the cliffs of Dover, as to penetrate such a mass." Although the Ross Ice Shelf blocked his hopes of reaching the South Magnetic Pole, it was a sensational discovery. It proved to be the birthplace of the strange, flat-topped icebergs that had long puzzled Antarctic explorers.

WINTERING OVER

After the Ross expedition, interest in the Antarctic declined. It seemed that whatever was beyond the ice had little or no value. Then on January 24, 1895, the Norwegian Henryk Johan Bull made the first confirmed landing on the Antarctic continental mainland at Cape Adare. All other landings had been made either on the Antarctic Peninsula or on offshore islands. This landing sparked renewed interest in the Antarctic. People again began to wonder what the interior of Antarctica was really like.

A Swedish group under Otto Nordenskjöld soon set sail for Antarctica. The expedition's ship, the *Antarctic,* put Nordenskjöld and five others ashore on Snow Hill Island in February 1902. Their goal was to spend the winter on the island in a prefabricated building. Despite the bitter cold and one raging blizzard after another, the men not only survived but collected valuable scientific data. Once spring arrived, Nordenskjöld and two other men headed across the ice to the mainland with two sleds and several dogs. By the end of their thirty-three-day journey, they had covered nearly 400 miles (644 kilometers).

Hardy Norwegians, British, and this Swedish expedition had confirmed that people could live through an Antarctic winter without going insane and that it was possible to explore deep into the interior of the continent. But the Swedes' adventure was far from finished. When Nordenskjöld and his two men returned to Snow Hill Island to await the arrival of the *Antarctic,* it was summer. But the ship never arrived. The pack ice, which had opened up the previous year, did not break up this time. Nordenskjöld and his men had to endure a second winter in Antarctica. So, too, did the crew of the *Antarctic,* which sank

*Ernest Shackleton (left) had almost unbelievable experiences in Antarctica.
In 1908 Shackleton led an expedition to Antarctica to reach the South Magnetic
Pole and the geographic South Pole. They sailed on the* Nimrod *(right).*

during efforts to reach Snow Hill Island. The crew was forced to
spend the winter on Paulet Island. Against all odds the men
found each other and were rescued by a ship from Argentina in
November 1903.

SEEKING THE POLES

In 1902 Ernest Shackleton joined an Antarctic expedition headed
by Robert Falcon Scott. Shackleton developed scurvy, however,
and was shipped back to England. The failure humiliated the
young man, but Shackleton was determined to prove himself
worthy of being an Antarctic explorer. In the coming years he
would do precisely that. In 1908 the bold and charismatic
Shackleton returned to Antarctica aboard the *Nimrod*. This time he
led his own expedition. His goals were to reach the South
Magnetic Pole as well as the geographic South Pole.

On his 1908 expedition, Shackleton successfully used ponies (left) instead of dogs. He stands at his winter quarters (right) with Mount Erebus in the background.

Shackleton, with Jameson Adams, Eric Marshall, and Frank Wild, would attempt to reach the geographic South Pole from their Cape Royds hut. Another team, under the command of fifty-year-old Edgeworth David, would set out for the South Magnetic Pole. In January 1909 David, along with Douglas Mawson and Alistair Mackay, hoisted the Union Jack (the British flag) at the South Magnetic Pole and claimed the area for the British Empire. The trip back to the *Nimrod* was a brutal struggle against the raw elements, but they survived. In all, the three explorers had walked 1,260 miles (2,028 kilometers) without assistance from dogs or ponies.

Such success, however, eluded Shackleton and his men. Their journey lasted 128 days, from October 29, 1908 to March 5, 1909. During that time they marched through snow so soft their Siberian ponies sank up to their bellies. The men discovered and climbed the 10,000-foot (3,048-meter) Beardmore Glacier. Several

The Shackleton party look into the crater of Mount Erebus.

times a member of the team fell into a crevasse only to be saved by the other members of the team. They killed their ponies one by one for food. Their last pony, named Socks, broke through a piece of thin snow crust on the Beardmore Glacier and fell into a crevasse so deep that the men could see neither Socks nor the bottom of the black pit.

Still, despite illness and near starvation, Shackleton and his men reached 88 degrees 23 minutes south latitude on January 9, 1909. That was the closest anyone had ever come to reaching the South Pole. They bettered the old record by 360 miles (579 kilometers) and were only 112 miles (180 kilometers) from their goal, but they were now too weak to go any farther. Growing weaker, and with so few provisions, they could only turn around and hope to make it back safely. Somehow, like David's team, they made it. Shackleton and his men had walked 1,700 miles (2,736 kilometers) across the coldest place on earth. For his heroic efforts, Shackleton won fame and was knighted by King Edward VII of England.

Chapter 6

THE RACE TO THE SOUTH POLE: TRIUMPH AND TRAGEDY

On April 6, 1909, Robert E. Peary and Matthew Henson achieved what no one ever had before. They stood together on the top of the earth at the North Pole. Although this claim has been widely debated, the news of their conquest electrified the world. Now only the South Pole was left to be conquered. By 1911 the Norwegians, Germans, Japanese, British, and Australians had expeditions in Antarctica. They all had the same goal—to reach the geographic South Pole first. Soon, however, the race was narrowed to Roald Amundsen of Norway and Robert F. Scott of Great Britain.

ROALD AMUNDSEN

Roald Amundsen was a seasoned explorer. He had already completed an impressive list of polar achievements. In 1897 he

Robert E. Peary (left) and Matthew Henson (right) are often named as the first explorers to have reached the North Pole.

took part in a Belgian expedition to Antarctica. Then in 1901 he conducted oceanographic research off the northeast coast of Greenland. Perhaps his greatest achievement came in 1905 when he became the first man to sail through the long-sought Northwest Passage and around the northern Canadian coast.

Amundsen, a determined and ambitious man, was planning to conquer the North Pole when he heard about Peary and Henson's feat. He saw no point in doing what had already been done. In this era of heroic exploration there was a great deal of national and personal pride to be won for being the first to achieve something. So Amundsen quickly altered his plans and headed for the South Pole. At first he kept his plans a secret. Even the eight members of his crew did not know the details until the last possible moment. Then, in the name of fairness to his chief rival, he informed Scott of his new plan. After he was well under way he sent a brief message to Scott: "Heading south. Amundsen."

Roald Amundsen (left), Robert Scott (center), and Scott's ship, the Terra Nova *(right)*

ROBERT F. SCOTT

Like Amundsen, Robert Scott was well prepared for an attempt to conquer the South Pole. Trained as a naval officer and scientist, this highly dedicated and disciplined man headed a three-year expedition to Antarctica from 1901 to 1904. He explored and named King Edward VII Land. Scott was also one of the first explorers to go beyond the rim of the polar plateau and into the interior. The polar plateau rises about 10,000 feet (3,048 meters) above sea level. The geographic South Pole is on the polar plateau.

Late in 1910 Scott set sail for Antarctica aboard the *Terra Nova*. He was confident that he would be the first man to reach the South Pole. When he received the message from Amundsen, Scott was shocked. He now knew that it would be a desperate race between both expeditions for the South Pole. Scott arrived at

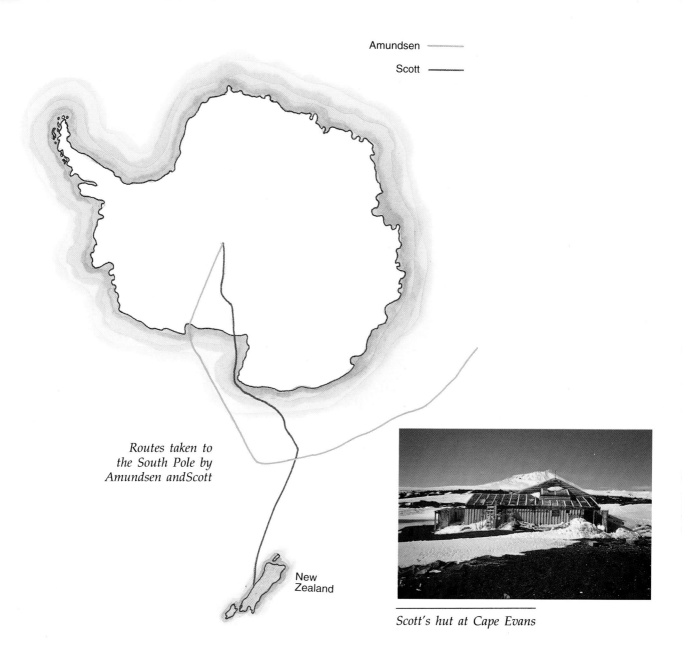

Amundsen ————
Scott ————

*Routes taken to
the South Pole by
Amundsen and Scott*

New
Zealand

Scott's hut at Cape Evans

McMurdo Sound on January 3, 1911. Eleven days later, Scott
received further bad news. He learned that Amundsen had set up
his base camp at the Bay of Whales on the Ross Ice Shelf, 400
miles (644 kilometers) farther east and 60 miles (97 kilometers)
closer to the South Pole than Scott's base camp.

Each of Amundsen's sleds were pulled by thirteen hardy Greenland huskies.

THE RACE IS ON

From the beginning, Amundsen realized that the slightest problem with either transportation or food could spell disaster. So he made absolutely certain that he had plenty of both. He and his four men used skis and four sleds, each pulled by thirteen hardy Greenland huskies. In addition, the Norwegians were expert dog-team handlers. The decision to use dogs was an important factor in Amundsen's success.

Scott, on the other hand, had to rely on human power to pull his sleds. He had Siberian ponies and experimental motor sleds, but the ponies soon became ill and the motor sleds could only be used around the base camp. Scott had earlier rejected the idea of using dogs. A deeply sensitive man, Scott disliked the way the Norwegians handled their dogs. They drove the dogs hard and then slaughtered them once they were no longer useful when sleds lightened during the journey.

Amundsen and Scott both set up food depots along their

intended routes. That, however, turned out to be the only similarity between the two expeditions. Things went smoothly for the Norwegians from the beginning. On October 20, 1911, they set out for the South Pole under a beautiful sky. The group was made up of Amundsen, Olav Olavsen Bjaaland, Helge Sverre Hassel, Oscar Wisting, and Helmer Julius Hanssen. They rode on their sleds for the first 100 miles (161 kilometers). The dogs then towed the men on their skis behind the sleds for the next 300 miles (483 kilometers). By the time the Norwegians reached the challenging mountain range (named the Queen Maud Mountains by Amundsen), they were still strong and well rested. After the men climbed to 10,750 feet (3,277 meters), Amundsen ordered all but the eighteen strongest dogs killed. The Norwegians then stored the meat for the return trip. From there the men traveled along at the brisk pace of 20 miles (32 kilometers) per day.

Finally, on December 14, 1911, Amundsen and his men reached the South Pole. Somehow it seemed appropriate that it was a bright, clear day. The Norwegians proudly planted their nation's flag at 90 degrees south. They also took some photographs. Amundsen named the flat plateau region around the South Pole King Haakon VII Plateau. He and his men stayed at the South Pole until December 17, so that they could study the area and make observations. Before leaving for an equally smooth trip back to the Bay of Whales, Amundsen left a note for Scott. He was sure the Englishman would be arriving at the pole soon.

A HEROIC STRUGGLE

Robert Scott's trip started out poorly, and things grew steadily worse. Before he even started, his Siberian ponies became ill and

Scott's party (left to right) included Bowers, Oates, Evans, Scott, and Wilson.

were of little use. Several of his men also became sick or were injured. Unlike Amundsen, Scott had to face a series of unusual summer blizzards. In his diary, which would become one of the great classics in the annals of exploration, Scott called the weather "wretched." Then, one week before he was ready to leave, Scott received word that Amundsen had already left the Bay of Whales and was headed for the South Pole. Scott was too conscientious an explorer to rush things. Knowing how important it was to be properly prepared, he decided to "act exactly as I should have done had he [Amundsen] not existed."

On November 1, 1911, Scott headed south from McMurdo Sound. The four men who were to go with him all the way to the South Pole were Edward Wilson, Lawrence Oates, Edgar Evans, and Henry Bowers. Scott's team first had to cross the Ross Ice Shelf and then climb the Beardmore Glacier to reach the polar plateau. From there it would be a 350-mile (563-kilometer) dash across the high plateau to the pole.

The Siberian ponies were left at the foot of the Beardmore Glacier, forcing the men to haul their own sleds. Successful trial runs had convinced Scott and his men that it could be done. No one, however, could have guessed just how bad the weather would get during this Antarctic summer. One raging blizzard kept them from moving on for four consecutive days. When the weather improved they pressed on, convinced that their discipline and will power would get them to the South Pole.

"NOT A HAPPY PARTY"

The trip was agonizingly slow. Some days they managed to travel only six or seven miles (ten or eleven kilometers). Pulling their own sleds began to take its toll. The men grew steadily weaker. Every day they battled hunger, frostbite, and the rugged terrain. Still, Scott and his men plodded bravely on toward their goal. On January 15, Scott wrote in his diary, "Only 27 miles from the Pole. We ought to make it now."

The next afternoon the men started out with high hopes. Suddenly, Bowers spotted a little speck on the horizon. What could it be? As Bowers wearily approached, the speck began to move. It was a black flag! It marked one of Amundsen's campsites. The shock of knowing that the Norwegians had arrived first cast a pall over the men. "We're not a very happy party tonight," said Oates.

Two days later, on January 18, 1912, the men arrived at the South Pole. There they found Amundsen's tent and note. Amundsen had left the note just in case he and his party suffered an accident on the return journey. It read:

Dear Captain Scott:
As you probably are the first to reach this area
after us, I will ask you kindly to forward this
letter to King Haakon VII. If you can use any of
the articles left in the tent please do not
hesitate to do so. With kind regards I wish you
a safe return.

Yours truly,
Roald Amundsen

THE TRAGIC END

Bitterly disappointed, Scott made a few scientific observations and set out for the trek back to Cape Evans on January 19, 1912. The return trip marked one of the most tragic tales in the history of human exploration. Food supplies were dangerously low. They had to struggle to make it from one food depot to the next. Evans badly injured himself when he fell while walking on a glacier. Slowly, his health deteriorated. During the night of February 17 he died in his sleep.

Oates developed such horrible frostbite that he could barely move. He knew that he was slowing down the other men. On March 17, during yet another blizzard, Oates told Scott that he was going outside the tent and would be gone for a while. He wandered off and was never seen again. Scott wrote, "We knew that poor Oates was walking to his death, but . . . we knew it was the act of a brave man and an English gentleman."

The remaining three men continued their journey. Now, however, they were pleased if they made five or six miles (eight or ten kilometers) per day. Finally, on March 21, the Antarctic

Scott's men before the end of their tragic return trip in 1912.

winter arrived with a fierce blizzard. For one week the men remained trapped inside their tent by the swirling snow. By now they knew that they could not possibly make it home. Bowers and Wilson wrote private notes to their families back in England. On March 29 Scott wrote, "I do not think we can hope for any better things now. We shall stick it out to the end, but we are getting weaker, of course, and the end cannot be far. It seems a pity, but I do not think I can write more."

Eight months later a search party found the tent and the three frozen bodies. Whereas Roald Amundsen gained fame as the first man to reach the South Pole, Robert Scott left a legacy of heroism for his expedition that met with failure.

Chapter 7

LATER EXPLORATION

Reaching the magnetic and geographic South Poles did not end the age of Antarctic exploration. You might say that such headline news was merely the tip of the iceberg. There was much work yet to be done. Only a very small percentage of the continent had been explored and accurately mapped when Roald Amundsen and his companions stood at the South Pole in 1911.

ERNEST SHACKLETON AND THE GLORIOUS FAILURE

During 1913 and 1914 Ernest Shackleton found financial backing for and planned what he called "the greatest Polar journey ever attempted." He wanted to walk across Antarctica from the Weddell Sea over the South Pole to the Ross Sea, a total of 1,800 miles (2,897 kilometers). "Every step," he promised, "will be an advance in geographical science."

TRAPPED IN THE ICE

On August 8, 1914, Shackleton and his men boarded the *Endurance* and set sail for the Weddell Sea. On December 11 the

Ernest Shackleton's ship, Endurance, *was gradually crushed in the ice.
The interior of Shackleton's hut at Cape Royds (inset)*

ship reached its goal and began weaving its way through unusually heavy and thick ice for that time of year. It was slow going. On January 19, 1915, the ice closed in and trapped the *Endurance.* At first, no one was terribly worried. It was still summer in the Antarctic and the men felt sure that a strong wind would soon break up the ice pack. But things did not work out that way.

The ice maintained its deathlike grip on the ship month after month. It was not until October that a wild blizzard began to break up the ice. This, however, caused more problems than it solved. As the ice cracked and opened, huge chunks were lifted into the air by other pieces moving beneath. By November 21, 1915, the trapped *Endurance* was slowly crushed like a child's toy by the enormous forces of the shifting ice and sank. As Shackleton wrote, "I cannot describe the impressions of relentless destruction . . . The floes . . . were simply annihilating the ship."

Shackleton's dream of an Antarctic crossing went down with the *Endurance*. The group now faced the challenge of survival, for Shackleton and his twenty-seven men were stranded on an ice floe hundreds of miles from land with no hope of being rescued. Fortunately, they had removed most of their supplies and the longboats from the *Endurance* before it sank. For several months the men drifted north on the ice. On April 9, 1916, as the floe began to break up in the warmer waters, Shackleton ordered his men into the two twenty-foot (six-meter) longboats. The sea and the wind were merciless. Huge waves pounded the boats and soaked the men as they sat shivering in their frozen clothes.

Then, on April 15, they reached Elephant Island. Most of the men were delighted. It was the first time in 485 days that they had set foot on solid ground. But Shackleton and Frank Wild, hardened veterans of polar exploration, knew better. The barren island would protect them for a while, but not forever. Worse, Elephant Island was off the usual track of whalers and sealers. No one would think of looking for them there.

AN IMPOSSIBLE VOYAGE

Shackleton then decided to take the greatest risk of his life. He had to go for help, but the nearest place was South Georgia, 800 miles (1,287 kilometers) across the stormiest seas on the earth. The men knew that it was nearly an impossible voyage, but it was their only hope. On Easter Monday, April 24, Shackleton, along with five volunteers, boarded the *James Caird*, one of the

Shackleton and five volunteers landed on the wrong side of South Georgia. They had to climb the mountains to reach the whaling station on the other side of the island. The whaling stations are no longer in use. These huge drums (below) were used to store whale oil.

longboats. Shackleton placed his trusted friend, Frank Wild, in command of the twenty-one other men left behind on Elephant Island—men who were to live beneath an upturned boat during the long wait to be rescued.

Shackleton's voyage was one of the most remarkable feats of seamanship in history. Somehow, despite raging storms, frozen limbs, almost no sleep, and a thirst that grew into "a burning pain," they made it. On May 8, 1916, they caught sight of South Georgia.

Their troubles were not yet over, for they landed on the wrong side of the island. The whaling station—and safety—were on the other side of South Georgia, 17 miles (27 kilometers) away.

A photograph taken after the Shackleton party was rescued includes (left to right): Frank Wild, Ernest Shackleton, Dr. Eric Marshall, and Jameson Adams.

Neither the boat nor the men were in any condition to go to sea again and sail around the island. Several men were too ill and weak even to move. The only other choice was to climb over a 6,000-foot (1,829-meter) mountain range to reach the whaling station. On May 19 Shackleton, along with Tom Crean and Frank Worsley, set off to climb over mountains that no one had ever climbed before. With no sleeping bags and only light clothing they had to keep moving night and day.

Somehow, once again, they made it. All the men at the whaling station knew who Shackleton was. But when they saw the three blackened and bearded strangers standing at the door, they did not recognize them. When asked his name, Shackleton quietly replied, "My name is Shackleton." With that, the men at the whaling station began to cry.

THE END OF THE HEROIC AGE

The next day the three men on the other side of South Georgia were rescued. Several months later, on August 30, 1916, the twenty-two men left on Elephant Island were rescued by the

Chilean steamer *Yelcho* after several failed attempts by different vessels. They had been stranded there for 105 days. Shackleton himself went along on the rescue ship. "Are you well?" he shouted when he saw the men.

"All safe!" Frank Wild yelled back. "All well!"

Of course, when it began, no one knew that Shackleton's expedition with the *Endurance* would not succeed. Not one of its men would even set foot on the continent. Yet the ship's captain, Frank Worsley, said, "Among all [Shackleton's] achievements, great as they were, his one failure was the most glorious."

Remarkably, not a single man died during this incredible ordeal which lasted, in total, nearly two years. In fact, Shackleton never lost a man during any of his Antarctic adventures. Shackleton himself was not so lucky. He died of heart failure on January 5, 1922, while sailing aboard the *Quest* on yet another Antarctic voyage. He was only forty-eight years old.

The sudden death of Ernest Shackleton during his fourth Antarctic expedition ended what is sometimes called the "heroic age" of Antarctic exploration. It was followed by the "mechanized age." Motorized vehicles and airplanes were introduced in the Antarctic. Permanent research stations replaced temporary base camps.

THE FIRST PLANE FLIGHTS

Between November 1928 and February 1929, the Australian Hubert Wilkins introduced the airplane to the Antarctic. On November 16, 1928, he took a short flight from Deception Island in a Lockheed Vega monoplane. It was the first time anyone had flown a plane in the Antarctic. Four days later he took off again

Left: Hubert Wilkins was photographed after he made the first polar flight over the North Pole from Alaska.
Right: Richard Byrd with the Fokker plane he used for his North Pole flight

for a longer flight over the Antarctic Peninsula. He covered 1,300 miles (2,092 kilometers) and saw terrain that no other human had ever seen. Wilkins went on to make several more flights, discovering, as he went, new terrain and some of the many hazards of polar flight.

RICHARD BYRD'S FLIGHT OVER THE SOUTH POLE

The most famous polar aviator of all time was Richard Evelyn Byrd. On May 9, 1926, this son of a famous Virginia family became the first person to fly over the North Pole. On his return to the United States he was given a hero's welcome in New York City. The Norwegian, Roald Amundsen, who was there to greet him, asked Byrd what his next goal was. Byrd half-jokingly answered, "The South Pole."

To most people the idea of flying over the South Pole was inconceivable. After all, only two expeditions had ever been to the

The Fokker plane Byrd used in Antarctica was fitted with specially made steel pontoons.

South Pole, and only one had lived to tell about it. Still, Byrd thought it could be done with proper preparation. When he finally headed to the Antarctic in 1928, he led the best-equipped, best-prepared polar expedition of his time. He had three planes, ninety-five dogs, and more than fifty men. The expedition reached the Ross Ice Shelf on December 25, 1928. Byrd found a suitable site for a landing strip just east of the Bay of Whales. There he and his men established their base with three buildings. Byrd called it Little America.

Byrd made his first Antarctic flight on January 15, 1929. He discovered a range of mountains and named them the Rockefeller Mountains. He also discovered what Wilkins had already learned about Antarctic flying. A regular compass proved to be useless. The needle spun wildly in all directions because the South Magnetic Pole was so near. The plane's engine oil had to be heated by torch before takeoff. The glare of the ice made it difficult to see. Distances in the vast and often featureless landscape were nearly impossible to judge. High crosswinds made taking off and landing very hazardous.

On November 28 everything was in place. Byrd was ready to try to fly over the South Pole with his three-engine Ford monoplane. This choice of plane, however, presented a problem. The Ford monoplane was large enough to carry important supplies such as fuel, emergency food, and heavy aerial camera equipment, but the load was too heavy. The Ford monoplane could not fly over the Queen Maud Mountains, which have peaks 15,000 feet (4,572 meters) high. With luck the plane could fly high enough to clear a mountain pass created by a glacier.

The Ford monoplane took off from Little America with four men: Richard Byrd, navigator; Bernt Balchen, pilot; Harold June, radio operator; and Ashley McKinley, photographer. The moment of truth came when they reached the end of the Ross Ice Shelf. Could they get their plane to fly high enough? Byrd had intended to fly up the Axel Heiberg Glacier but, at the last moment, saw clouds near it and chose the Liv Glacier instead.

The winds tossed the plane about as Balchen tried to squeeze more altitude out of it. It was no use. He shouted to Byrd that they would have to discharge some weight or turn back. Byrd decided to dispose of some food. After this the plane gained altitude, but not enough. "Dump more!" shouted Balchen.

Another huge sack of food went out the trapdoor. Just when it seemed the plane would crash into the glacier, it lifted once again and cleared the Liv Glacier with only a few feet to spare. From there it was smooth sailing across the ice cap. At 1:14 A.M. on November 29 the plane reached the South Pole. In all, the flight lasted 15 hours and 51 minutes. It had taken Amundsen three months to reach the same goal overland. The face of Antarctic

Left: Rear Admiral Byrd discussed the navy's Antarctic expedition at a Pentagon news conference in 1956. Right: A base used during Operation Highjump in 1947

exploration had changed forever. Richard Byrd had seen more of Antarctica in one flight than Amundsen and Scott had seen during all their years. From that moment on, the continent would be mapped and explored primarily from the air.

FURTHER BYRD EXPLOITS

Richard Byrd's work in Antarctica was far from finished. In 1934 he wintered alone at the Bolling Advance Weather Station, 123 miles (198 kilometers) south of Little America. Byrd wanted to see what that experience would be like. He nearly did not survive. Carbon monoxide fumes from his stove and a faulty electrical generator nearly proved fatal before he was rescued.

Byrd's exploits helped to stimulate the interest of the U.S. government in polar exploration. Byrd led a U.S. expedition from 1939 to 1941. Then, from 1946 to 1947, he headed Operation Highjump, a U.S. naval expedition that was larger than all previous expeditions combined. It involved thirteen ships, twenty-

Douglas Mawson (left) and eight of his party were marooned in this hut (right) for more than a week on Heard Island before they were rescued.

three planes, and more than forty-seven hundred men. During this operation icebreakers were used in Antarctica for the first time. Finally, during 1955-1956, Byrd was put in charge of Operation Deepfreeze. He made his last trip to Antarctica in December 1955. He was sixty-eight years old at the time. This great man, who pioneered the use of modern vehicles and communications for polar exploration, died two years later.

OTHER NOTABLE FIRSTS

Douglas Mawson of Australia was another courageous explorer from the heroic age. He was a member of Edgeworth David's party, the first to climb Mount Erebus and reach the South Magnetic Pole. In 1912 and 1913 Mawson survived the death of his two companions and crossed George V Land alone. Then from

Left: Lincoln Ellsworth (left) and Herbert Hollick-Kenyon
(right) made the first flight across Antarctica. Right: Vivian
Fuchs used Sno-cats to cross the continent.

1929 to 1931 he led an expedition that discovered MacRobertson
Land, the Banzare Coast, and Princess Elizabeth Land.

In November 1935, a U.S. explorer named Lincoln Ellsworth
and an Englishman named Herbert Hollick-Kenyon made the first
flight across the continent of Antarctica. They flew from Dundee
Island in the Weddell Sea to Little America on the Bay of Whales,
a distance of 2,300 miles (3,701 kilometers), in a single-engine
plane. Unfortunately, the plane ran out of fuel just short of their
final destination. They landed safely, however, and walked the rest
of the way. They reached Little America on December 15, 1935,
twenty-two days after their takeoff on a flight that was supposed
to last only fourteen hours. The land discovered on this flight
became known as Ellsworth Land.

In 1958 the Englishman Vivian Fuchs, as the leader of the
Commonwealth Trans-Antarctic expedition, completed the first

overland continental crossing. With Sno-cats, special vehicles used to travel over snow surfaces, and massive support Fuchs completed the journey in ninety-nine days, forty-four years after Ernest Shackleton's attempt.

WOMEN IN ANTARCTICA

What role did women play during the early days of Antarctic exploration? The wives of explorers typically remained at home. Often they did not see or hear from their husbands for months or even years at a time. While Ernest Shackleton was involved with his epic attempt to cross Antarctica, Emily Shackleton did not see him for more than two years. Kathleen Scott did not even learn about her husband's death until 1913, more than a year after Robert Scott and his men died on their return from the South Pole.

Gradually things began to change as women began to take part in Antarctic adventures. In 1935 the wife of a whaling factory ship captain, Caroline Mikkelsen, was the first woman to step on the Antarctic continent. In 1947 Edith Ronne and Jennie Darlington spent a year living and working with their husbands on Stonington Island near the Antarctic Peninsula. They were the first women to live in Antarctica. (The Ronne Ice Shelf was originally named Edith Ronne Land.) It took a while for men to accept the presence of women in the Antarctic, but gradually most of them have. Women scientists and support staff now have worked on equal terms with men at most Antarctic research stations. Some women have worked or may currently work as station managers.

Chapter 8

COOPERATION
AMONG NATIONS

The exploration of Antarctica did not occur in a political or historical vacuum. At the same time Antarctic heroes were risking their lives on the frozen continent, the rest of the earth was experiencing the events of the first half of the twentieth century, one of the most war torn in human history. For example, at the same time that Ernest Shackleton and his men were struggling to survive in the Antarctic, millions of people were dying in World War I. Tens of millions more died during World War II. In addition, the first half of the twentieth century included bitter struggles for independence, countless border disputes, and smaller wars of every description.

In short, the years from 1900 to 1950 were riddled with bitter international conflicts. What would all this mean for the future of Antarctica? Seven nations had made territorial claims on the continent. Some of these claims overlapped each other. Five other nations that engaged in polar exploration made no land claims for themselves, but ignored the claims of those that had. By the 1950s the situation appeared ripe for conflict. Fortunately, common sense prevailed. Nations agreed to put their territorial claims on hold while sharing scientific information. To date, overall, the nations of the world have behaved remarkably well in Antarctica.

RIVAL CLAIMS

Disputes arose from the earliest days of discovery in Antarctica. These sometimes led to confusion over different names given to the same place. The Antarctic Peninsula is a case in point. The Chileans called it O'Higgins Land (*Tierra O'Higgins*) after their national hero Bernardo O'Higgins. The Argentines named it San Martín Land (*Tierra San Martín*) after their revolutionary leader José de San Martín. People in the United States called it Palmer Peninsula after Nathaniel Palmer, who discovered the South Orkney Islands. To the English it became known as Graham Land, named after an English lord. Today the northern half of the peninsula is called Graham Land and the southern half is called Palmer Land. The region taken as a whole is known as the Antarctic Peninsula.

Between 1908 and 1942 seven nations claimed pie-shaped sections covering approximately 85 percent of the Antarctic continent: Australia, New Zealand, France, Norway, the United Kingdom, Argentina, and Chile. Five of these countries–France, New Zealand, Australia, Norway, and the United Kingdom–recognized each other's claims. Chile and Argentina, however, challenged the British claim as well as each other's because they overlapped. Other nations, including the United States, the Soviet Union, Japan, Belgium, and Germany, all made discoveries in the Antarctic but did not assert any formal claims.

Australia's claim over 42 percent of the continent is the largest. The United States and the Soviet Union, however, reserved the right to make a claim at some point in the future.

INTERNATIONAL POLAR YEARS

The Antarctic region has become a model for world peace and cooperation. The first step on the long road to polar cooperation began in 1875 when Karl Weyprecht, an Austrian naval officer, proposed that the various national scientific programs in both the Arctic and Antarctic be coordinated. Twelve nations agreed to participate in the first International Polar Year of 1882-1883. Most of the work was done in the Arctic. Of the fourteen stations set up in the polar regions to observe the climate and the earth's magnetism, only one, a German station on South Georgia, was near the Antarctic. The effort was repeated during the second International Polar Year of 1932-1933.

THE INTERNATIONAL GEOPHYSICAL YEAR, 1957-1958

The original plan was to organize an international polar year every fifty years, but things began to change on April 5, 1950, at the Maryland home of U.S. physicist James Van Allen. The dinner guests that evening included Doctor Lloyd Berkner, a member of Richard Byrd's 1928-1930 expedition. Berkner wondered why scientists had to wait so long to explore the upper atmosphere and the earth's surface when they already had new technologies that had not existed in 1933. All the other scientists present agreed, and Berkner's idea was sent to the International Council of Scientific Unions (ICSU).

The ICSU, which represented sixty-seven nations, approved the idea and set up a special committee called the Comité Spéciál de l'Année Geophysique Internationale (CSAGI) to coordinate planning for future research. It was agreed that the third polar year, now known as the International Geophysical Year (IGY), would take place from July 1, 1957 to December 31, 1958, to coincide with peak sunspot activity that would be observable in the region.

This time the research involved more than the polar regions and the atmosphere. It included the entire surface of the earth and the ocean depths as well. Representatives from twelve nations planning research in the Antarctic during the IGY met in Paris in July 1955 to discuss how they might help each other in terms of locating and building bases, launching rescue operations, setting up communication systems, sharing weather reports, and the like. After a mildly tense beginning, it was agreed that the focus of the IGY would be on science, not politics. Things went smoothly after that.

Twelve nations–Argentina, Australia, Belgium, Chile, France, Japan, New Zealand, Norway, South Africa, the United Kingdom, the United States, and the Soviet Union–conducted research in Antarctica during the IGY and set up Antarctic base camps in many different locations, some of which are still in use today. Antarctica was a busy place during the IGY, as dozens of new scientific stations were constructed on the mainland and various nearby islands. Scientists studied such topics as the pull of gravity, glaciology, cosmic rays, geomagnetism, and the *aurora australis,* or southern lights. It was also during the IGY that Vivian Fuchs completed his historic journey across the continent.

The United States built six facilities in Antarctica during the

Some of the personnel at McMurdo Station, operated by the United States, include a scientist who grows tomatoes in a nutrient solution rather than soil (top inset) and specially trained people who work at the weather station (bottom inset).

IGY, including a huge support station at McMurdo Sound, Byrd Station in Marie Byrd Land, Ellsworth Station on the Filchner Ice Shelf, and one at the geographic South Pole named after Amundsen and Scott. The Soviet Union also wanted to build a base at the geographic South Pole. Since the United States made the first request for that location, however, the Soviet Union stepped aside and built a base at the South Magnetic Pole instead. The Soviet Union also built a station at the Pole of Inaccessibility, the farthest point from all Antarctic coasts.

The flow of new scientific knowledge was truly staggering, but perhaps the greatest achievement of the International Geophysical Year was political, not scientific. Never before had so many nations worked together with such a spirit of cooperation on such a massive scale. Things went so well, in fact, that the nations agreed to continue their scientific cooperation in Antarctica

An aerial view of the Australian's Davis Station (above) and weather tracking equipment at Russia's Bellinghausen Station on King George Island (inset)

indefinitely. To help in this effort, the Scientific Committee on Antarctic Research (SCAR) was set up to serve as a scientific advisory body to the countries involved in Antarctica.

THE ANTARCTIC TREATY

When the IGY ended in 1958, some people worried that political disputes over Antarctica might arise once again. The U.S. Department of State acted quickly and set up meetings with the other eleven nations having Antarctic interests. Representatives met in Washington, D.C., for more than a year to iron out the details. These negotiations resulted in the Antarctic Treaty that was signed on December 1, 1959 by the twelve nations involved in Antarctica during the IGY. After each country ratified the treaty, it entered into force on June 23, 1961. Many other countries have since signed the treaty. As of April 1994 forty-two countries were bound by the treaty. The current spirit of cooperation remains essential to the future of Antarctica.

The preamble to the Antarctic Treaty clearly sets forth its purpose:

> Recognizing that it is in the interest of all
> mankind that Antarctica shall continue forever
> to be used exclusively for peaceful purposes
> and shall not become the scene or object of
> international discord; . . . the establishment
> of a firm foundation for the continuation
> and development of such co-operation on the
> basis of freedom of scientific investigation in
> Antarctica as applied during the International
> Geophysical Year accords with the interests of
> science and the progress of all mankind. . . .

The treaty parties agreed to put aside their territorial claims indefinitely. The treaty also achieved several other remarkable feats. It placed a ban on military activity and weapons testing in the region. It called for international cooperation and freedom of scientific investigation. The treaty promotes the free exchange of science program plans, results, and personnel and entitles treaty parties to open inspections of each other's facilities at all times without prior notice. Under the provisions of the treaty there can be no nuclear testing or disposal of radioactive wastes in Antarctica. In effect, this sets aside 10 percent of the earth as a nuclear-free, demilitarized zone. Treaty parties also agreed that disputes that cannot be settled by negotiation or arbitration are to be settled by the International Court of Justice. The Antarctic Treaty was designed to be flexible in order to deal with new issues or problems that might arise once it entered into force.

There are four official treaty languages: English, French, Russian, and Spanish. The United States government serves as the depository for treaty documents.

The Antarctic Treaty parties adopted the Agreed Measures for the Conservation of Antarctic Fauna and Flora in 1964. Other important instruments that govern Antarctica along with the treaty itself include the Convention for the Conservation of Antarctic Seals (CCAS), the Convention on the Conservation of Antarctic Marine Living Resources (CCAMLR), and many recommendations enacted by treaty parties to cover Antarctic activities. These instruments make up the Antarctic Treaty System (ATS).

In addition, in 1991 Antarctic Treaty parties signed the Protocol on Environmental Protection to the Antarctic Treaty, which must be ratified by all parties before it enters into force. Its goal is to help preserve the environment. When the original treaty was signed, environmental awareness was very limited; therefore, environmental protection was not a priority. It has since become one. Environmental groups have called attention to the waste management practices in place at Antarctic scientific research stations and other environmental issues in Antarctica. Among the most active nongovernment organizations (NGOs) in Antarctica are Greenpeace and The Antarctica Project.

Today scientists are more careful about the way they treat the environment. Under the 1991 Protocol, treaty parties pledged to regulate their behavior to protect the region's ecosystems. The protocol bans all exploration and mining of natural resources on the continent for at least the next fifty years. The protocol requires treaty parties to conduct environmental impact assessments for their planned activities. All countries must enact laws to require that citizens observe the provisions of the protocol.

Chapter 9

IMPORTANT CURRENT
AND FUTURE ISSUES

Tourism and fishing represent the two commercial industries currently operating in Antarctica. These and other issues challenge the governments that oversee Antarctica and its special environment.

MINERAL RESOURCES

Scientists have only a partial picture of what mineral resources may be stored within Antarctica because so much of the continent is buried under an average thickness of more than one mile (1.6 kilometers) of ice. But if Antarctica is similar to the mineral-rich regions of nearby continents, it probably has its fair share of mineral resources such as coal, iron, copper, gold, and oil.

The technology exists to remove whatever minerals might be found, but at present it is not considered to be economically feasible. Transportation costs, for example, would be very high because the continent is so far from major world markets and because icebreakers and specially equipped airplanes would be

Seismic instruments used to study Mount Erebus (above),
a Lockheed C-130 Hercules equipped with skis for landing
(top right), and a radio transmitter used for tracking seals
(bottom right) are some of the specialized equipment
used in Antarctica.

needed. Also, polar workers might have to be paid higher wages
than similar workers in more temperate climates. Then there are
environmental concerns. Imagine how difficult and costly it would
be to stop a leak on an oil tanker hit by an iceberg or leaks on an
offshore oil well during a blizzard, extreme cold snap, or months
of darkness. The exploitation of mineral resources might also have
a major effect on marine plants and animals. Scientists are just
beginning to understand the Antarctic ecosystems. Some may be
very fragile.

TOURISM

Antarctic tourism is increasing. More than seventy-two hundred
tourists visited Antarctica during the 1992-1993 austral (southern
hemisphere) summer. In comparison, roughly four thousand
science and support personnel work in Antarctica each year. With
its mountains, wildlife, glaciers, ice shelves, dry valleys, icebergs,

The United States Amundsen-Scott station at the geographic South Pole (left) and some of the waste generated at the United States station at McMurdo Sound (inset)

caused by the burning of fossil fuels that results in air pollution. In turn, this pollution blocks the escape of heat energy from the earth. Even a small change in the earth's average temperatures would cause some melting of the Antarctic ice cap. If enough ice were to melt, the earth's oceans would rise considerably, flooding many cities and lowland areas. In addition, the polar regions are the engines that drive the world's weather system. These are only some of the many reasons why research at the poles is so important.

Today scientists continue their studies in Antarctica. During the summer months approximately twelve hundred people work at McMurdo Station. Run by the United States, it is the largest research station in Antarctica. During the long winter, the number drops to approximately two hundred. The United States also operates Amundsen-Scott South Pole Station at 90 degrees south. There, scientists live and work in buildings housed inside a huge geodesic dome designed to protect them from high winds. The

Poland's Arctowski Station on King George Island

United States National Science Foundation (NSF) oversees the United States Antarctic Program (USAP). Scientists from all over the country compete to obtain funding that will allow them to conduct their research projects.

Many other nations also run year-round research stations in the Antarctic, including Argentina, Australia, Brazil, Chile, China, France, Germany, India, Japan, New Zealand, People's Republic of Korea, Poland, Russia, South Africa, the United Kingdom, and Uruguay. Many research stations are located along the Antarctic Peninsula. Scientific work varies at each station: some specialize in biological research; many serve as weather stations; still others study upper atmospheric physics.

A geologist ponders the Transantarctic Mountains

LOOKING AHEAD

Some people view Antarctica as the earth's last great wilderness. Some believe the continent hides an untold wealth of resources and information that will gradually come to light as scientists unlock secrets in biology, meteorology, and other branches of science. Antarctica may well be earth's last great science laboratory. As such, the nations of the world need to cooperate to protect the unique Antarctic environment. United States Vice-President Albert Gore has said that Antarctica "should be held in trust as a global ecological reserve for all the people of the world, not just in this generation, but later generations to come as well."

MAP KEY

Adare, Cape	F2
Adelaide Island	B2
Adélie Coast	G3
Admiralty Mountains	F2
Agassiz, Cape	B2
Albert Markham, Mount	E3
Alexander Island	B2, C2
American Highland	E5
Amery Ice Shelf	E5, F5
Amundsen Bay	D6
Amundsen Sea	D1
Amundsen-Scott (U. S.)	D3
Ann, Cape	D6, E6
Antarctic Circle	B1, B2, B3, B4, B5, C1, C5, C6, D6, E6, F1, F5, F6, G1, G2, G3, G4, G5
Antarctic Peninsula	A2, B2, C2
Anvers Island	B2
Arctowski (Poland)	A2
Asuka (Japan)	C5
Atlantic Indian Basin	A4, A5, B5 B6, C6
Atlantic Ocean	A4, A5, A6, B5, B6, C6
Balchen Glacier	E1
Balleny Basin	G1, G2
Balleny Islands	G2
Banzare Coast	G3, G4
Barne Inlet	E3, F3
Barrier Bay	F5
Bay of Whales	E2
Bear Island	D1
Beardmore Glacier	E3
Beaver Glacier	D6, E6
Beethoven Peninsula	C2
Belgica Mountains	D5
Belgrano II (Argentina)	C3
Bellingshausen (Russia)	A2
Bellingshausen Sea	C1
Berkner Island	C3
Berlin, Mount	E1
Bickerton, Cape	G3
Biscoe Islands	B2
Boothby, Cape	E6
Borg Mountain	C4
Bowman Island	G5
Bouvetoya (Nor.)	A6
Boyd Glacier	E2
Brabant Island	B2
Bransfield Strait	A2, B2
Breid Bay	C5
Britannia Range	F3
Bryan Coast	C2
Buckley Bay	G2, G3
Budd Coast	G4
Bunger Hills	G5
Burke Island	D1
Bursey, Mount	E1
Byrd Glacier	F2, F3
Caird Coast	C3, C4
Candlemas Islands	A4
Capitán Arturo Prat (Chile)	A2
Casey (Australia)	G4
Casey Bay	D6
Charcot Island	B2
Chelyuskintsy Ice Tongue	F6
Clarence Island	A2
Clarie Coast	G3
Coats Land	C3, C4
Colbeck, Cape	E2
Coman, Mount	C2
Comandante Ferraz (Brazil)	A2
Commonwealth Bay	G3
Commonwealth Range	E3
Cook Ice Shelf	G2, G3
Coronation Island	A3
Coulman Island	F2
Crary Mountains	D1, D2
Dakshin Gangotri (India)	C5
Dalton Iceberg Tongue	G4
Darnley, Cape	E6
Dart, Cape	D1
Davis (Australia)	F5
Davis Bay	G3
Davis Sea	F5
Dawson-Lambton Glacier	C3
Deakin Bay	G2
Deception Island	A2
Denman Glacier	F5, G5
Dibble Iceberg Tongue	G3
Dodson Peninsula	C2, C3
Drake Passage	A1
Drygalski Island	F5
Dumont D'Urville (France)	G3
East Scotia Basin	A3
Edward VII Peninsula	E2
Edward VIII Bay	E6
Egerton, Mount	F3
Eights Coast	C1, C2
Elephant Island	A2
Ellsworth Land	C2
Ellsworth Mountains	C2
Enderby Land	D5, D6, E5, E6
English Coast	C2
Erebus, Mount	F2
Esperanza (Argentina)	A2
Eternity Range	B2
Executive Committee Range	D1, D2, E1, E2
Faraday (U.K.)	B2
Filchner Ice Shelf	C3
Fisher Glacier	E5
Fletcher Islands	C1
Flood Range	E1
Ford Ranges	E1, E2
Framnes Mountains	E5, E6
Fridtjof Nansen, Mount	E3
General Bernardo O'Higgins (Chile)	A2
Georg Forster (Ger.)	C5
Georg Von Neumayer (Ger.)	B4
George V Coast	G3
George VI Sound	B2, C2
Getz Ice Shelf	D1, E1
Glossopteris, Mount	D2
Graham Land	B2
Great Wall (China)	A2
Gribb Bank	G6
Grove Mountains	E5
Guest Peninsula	E1
Habermehl Peak	C5
Hallett, Cape	F2
Halley (U.K.)	C3
Hawkes, Mount	D3
Hearst Island	B2
Heritage Range	D2
Hobbs Coast	E1
Hollick-Kenyon Plateau	D2
Horlick Mountains	D2, E2
Hudson Mountains	C1, C2, D1, D2
Huggins, Mount	F2, F3
Hull Glacier	E1
Humboldt Mountains	C5
Ingrid Christensen Coast	F5
Jackson, Mount	B2
James Ross Island	A2
Jason Peninsula	B2
Joinville Island	A2
Jones Mountains	C1, C2
Kemp Coast	E6
Kemp Peninsula	C2
Kerguelen-Gaussberg Ridge	F6
King George Island	A2
Kirkpatrick, Mount	E3
Knox Coast	G4, G5
Kottas Mountains	C4
Kraul Mountains	C4
Kreitzer Glacier	E5
Lambert Glacier	E5
Larsen Ice Shelf	B2
Latady Island	C2
Laurie Island	A3
Lauritzen Bay	G2
Leningradskaja (Russia)	G2
Leopold and Astrid Coast	F5
Leskov Island	A4
Leverett Glacier	E2
Levick, Mount	F2
Livingston Island	A2
Lutpold Coast	C3
Lutzow-Holm Bay	D5, D6
Mac. Robertson Land	E5, E6
MacKenzie Bay	E6
Marambio (Argentina)	A2, B2
Marguerite Bay	B2
Marie Byrd Land	D1, D2
Markham, Mount	E3
Martin Peninsula	D1
Masson Island	G5
Matusevich Glacier	G2
Mawson (Australia)	E6
Mawson Escarpment	E5
Mawson Peninsula	G2
McClintock, Mount	F3
McMurdo (U.S.)	F2
McMurdo Sound	F2
Mellor Glacier	E5
Menzies, Mount	E5
Mertz Glacier Tongue	G3
Mikhaylov, Cape	G4
Mill Island	G5
Minna Bluff	F2
Mirny (Russia)	F5
Molodeznaja (Russia)	D6
Montagu Island	A4
Muhlig-Hofmann Mountains	C4, C5
Napier Mountains	E6
New Schwabenland	C4
Nimrod Glacier	E3
Ninnis Glacier Tongue	G3
Norths Highland	G4
Norvegia, Cape	B4
Novolazarevskaja (Russia)	C5
Oates Coast	G2
Ob'Bay	G2
Okuma Bay	E2
Orcadas (Argentina)	A3
Pacific Ocean	F1, G1, G2
Palmer (U.S.)	B2
Palmer Land	B2, C2
Paulding Bay	G4
Peacock Sound	C1, D1
Penck Trough	C4
Pensacola Mountains	D3
Peter Island	C1
Petras, Mount	D1
Philipi Glacier	F5, F6
Pine Island Bay	D1
Pobeda Ice Island	G5
Poinsett, Cape	G4
Polar Record Glacier	E5, F5
Porpoise Bay	G4
Possession Island	F2
Prestrud Inlet	E2
Prince Albert Mountains	F2, F3
Prince Charles Mountains	E5
Prince Olav Coast	D5, D6
Princess Astrid Coast	C5
Princess Martha Coast	C4
Princess Ragnhild Coast	C5, D5
Prydz Bay	F5
Queen Alexandra Range	E3
Queen Fabiola Mountains	D5
Queen Mary Coast	G5
Queen Maud Land	C4, C5, D4, D5
Queen Maud Mountains	E3
Rayner Glacier	D5, D6
Recovery Glacier	C3
Renaud Island	B2
Rennick Glacier	G2
Rennick Glacier	G2
Rex, Mount	C2
Riiser-Larsen Peninsula	D5, D6
Ritscher Upland	C4
Robertson Bay	F2
Rockefeller Plateau	D2, E2
Ronne Entrance	C2
Ronne Ice Shelf	C2, C3
Roosevelt Island	E2
Roscoe Glacier	F5
Ross Ice Shelf	E2, E3, F2, F3
Ross Island	F2
Ross Sea	F2
Rothera (U.K.)	B2
Sabine, Mount	F2
Sabrina Coast	G4
San Martin (Argentina)	B2
SANAE (South Africa)	C4
Saunders Island	A4
Scotia Ridge	A3
Scott Base (N.Z.)	F2
Scott Glacier	E2
Scott Glacier	G5
Seal Bay	B4
Sentinel Range	C2
Shackleton Glacier	E3
Shackleton Ice Shelf	G5
Shackleton Range	C3
Shepard Island	D1, E1
Shirase Glacier	D5
Sidley, Mount	D1
Signy (U.K.)	A3
Siple, Mount	D1
Siple Coast	E2
Slessor Glacier	C3, C4
Smith Island	A2
Smith Peninsula	C2
Smyley, Cape	C2
Sor Rondane Mountains	C5, D5
South Magnetic Pole	G3
South Orkney Islands	A3
South Pole	D3
South Sandwich Islands (U.K.)	A4
South Sandwich Trench	A3, A4
South Shetland Islands	A2
Stephenson, Mount	B2
Stinear Nunataks (peak)	E5
Sturge Island	G2
Sulzberger Bay	E2
Syowa (Japan)	D6
Takahe, Mount	D1
Teniente Rodolfo Marsh (Chile)	A2
Terra Nova Bay	F2
Theron Mountains	C3
Thiel Mountains	D2, D3
Thomas Mountains	C2
Thurston Island	C1
Thwaites Ice Tongue	D1
Totten Glacier	G4
Transantarctic Mountains	D3, E3, F2, F3, G2
Ulmer, Mount	C2
Usarp Mountains	F2, G2
Vahsel Bay	C3
Vang, Mount	C2
Victoria Land	F2
Vincennes Bay	G4, G5
Vinson Massif (peak)	C2, D2
Visokoi Island	A4
Vorterkaka Nunatak (peak)	D5
Vostok (Russia)	F4
Voyeykov Ice Shelf	G4
Wade, Mount	E3
Walgreen Coast	C1, D1
Ward, Mount	B2, C2
Weddell Sea	B2, B3, B4
West Ice Shelf	F5, F6
West Scotia Basin	A2
White Island	D6
Whitmore Mountains	D2
Wideroe, Mount	C5
Wilkes Land	F4, G3, G4
Wilkins Sound	B2, C2
Williams, Cape	G2
Williamson Head	G2
Wohlthat Mountains	C5
Wrigley Gulf	D1
Yule Bay	G2
Zhongshan (China)	F5

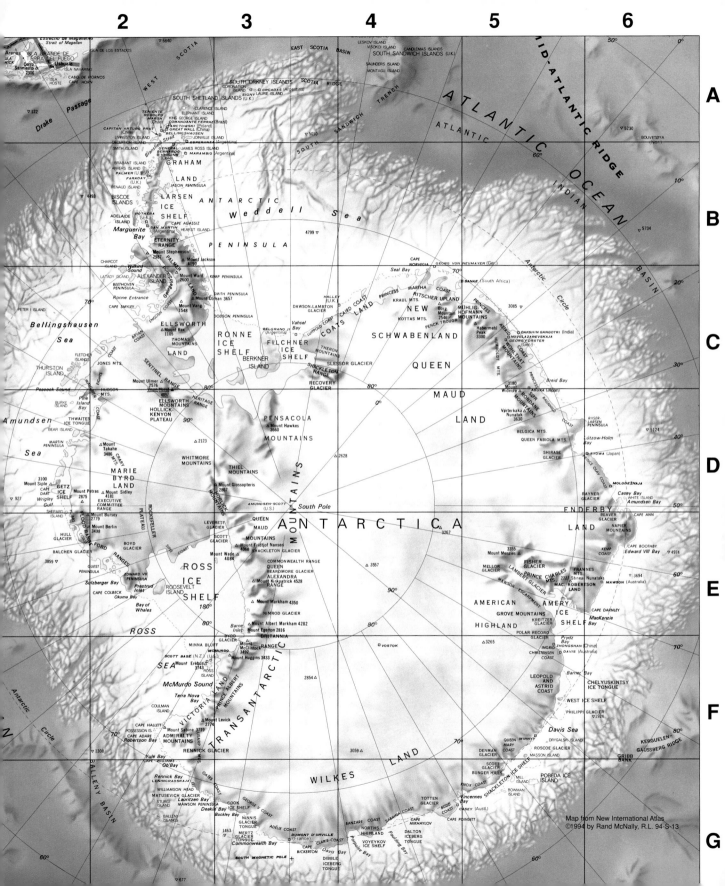

MINI-FACTS AT A GLANCE

GENERAL INFORMATION

ANTARCTIC FEATURES AND FACTS

Antarctic Convergence: A 25-mi. (40-km) wide irregular belt of water that serves as a biological boundary between 50 degrees and 60 degrees south latitude; here the cold Antarctic waters meet the warmer waters of the Atlantic, Pacific, and Indian Oceans. The temperature and chemical composition of the ocean are different on either side of the convergence, and this affects the species of birds and marine life.

Calving: The process of huge chunks of ice or icebergs breaking off from ice shelves and ice sheets.

Climate: More than 90 percent of the earth's permanent ice is found in Antarctica. The Antarctic ice sheet is the earth's largest storehouse of freshwater, containing some 68 percent of the earth's freshwater. The coastal regions are generally warmer than the interior; the Antarctic Peninsula is the warmest part of the continent. Due to its location, some parts of Antarctica have six months of continuous daylight from mid-September to mid-March and six months of continuous darkness from mid-March to mid-September, but there is prolonged twilight even at the South Pole. Most other areas have fewer than six months of continuous light or darkness each year.

Mean summer temperatures along most of the coast average 32° F. (0° C). In the interior, the mean summer temperatures range between -4° and -31° F. (-20° and -35° C). Winter temperatures in the interior rarely get much warmer than -40° F. (-40° C). The lowest temperature ever recorded was -129.3° F. (-89.6° C) at Vostok Station in 1983. Icy winds make the Antarctic air feel even colder. Commonwealth Bay is the windiest place on earth, where winds often blow between 50 mi. (80 km) and 90 mi. (145 km) per hour for several days in a row. There are, on average, eight to ten blizzards a year, each lasting for several days.

Antarctica is the driest continent on the earth. In the interior less than 2 in. (5 cm.) of precipitation falls annually. More precipitation falls along the coasts and can average 10 to 20 in. (25 to 51 cm) per year. Raging cyclones make the Southern Ocean the stormiest sea to be found anywhere on the earth.

Flag: One of the many unique characteristics of Antarctica is that it has no official flag of its own. To emphasize the continent's importance for humankind in such matters as scientific knowledge, exploration, and natural resources, the Flag Research Center of Winchester, Massachusetts, developed a distinctive Antarctic flag in 1985.

The emblem on the flag includes the first letter of the continent's name and a silhouette resembling the "bottom of the earth" as shown on a typical globe (the area southward from 60 degrees south latitude, which encompasses Antarctica). That area and the A above, suggesting one of the pair of scales traditionally held by Justice, remind countries of their need to deal justly with Antarctica and with each other. Below are stylized hands that symbolize protection of the fragile Antarctic environment. The need for guaranteed conditions of peace is suggested by the dove in the area that appears between the hands and the bottom segment of the globe. The background of the flag is "international orange," a color widely used in Antarctica because of its high visibility at a distance.

Katabatic winds: Fierce downflowing winds along the steep slopes of the interior highlands. They often sweep across ice caps and glaciers on subantarctic islands.

Nunataks: Mountain peaks that thrust through the ice and snow cover.

Ozone "hole": As the ozone layer over Antarctica erodes, an ozone "hole" develops each year between August and October.

Pack ice: Ice formed from seawater; pack ice forms a belt approximately 300 mi. to 1,800 mi. (483 km to 2,897 km) wide encircling the Antarctic continent in winter.

Permanent ice shelves: Floating slabs of ice jutting out from the coast; they form the boundaries between the ice sheet and the ice front.

Pollution: Winter Quarters Bay is one of the most polluted places on the continent. The bay served as a dumping ground for McMurdo Station until the late 1970s. Some water is still being discharged into it today. The water and bottom sediments are still contaminated.

Population: There are no indigenous inhabitants in Antarctica, but since 1944 many scientists and support personnel have lived and worked at research stations. Roughly 4,000 science and support personnel work in Antarctica each year. During the summer months approximately 1,200 people work at McMurdo Station, the largest U.S. base in Antarctica. During winter months the number of personnel at McMurdo Station drops to about 200.

Territorial claims: Seven nations–Argentina, Australia, Chile, France, New Zealand, Norway, and the United Kingdom–have made territorial claims on the continent. These claims may not be recognized by other countries, by the United Nations, or by other international bodies. Other original treaty signatory nations, which included the United States, the Soviet Union, Japan, Belgium, and South Africa, have not asserted any formal claims. The United States and the former Soviet Union reserved the right to make a claim at some point in the future. In 1991 the Soviet Union was dissolved into 15 separate states or nations. Eleven of the states formed the Commonwealth of Independent States (CIS). The largest of these states is the Russian Federation. Russia has taken the place of the former Soviet Union as a party to the Antarctic Treaty. The Antarctic Treaty froze all territorial claims, which means there is free access for all people throughout the continent.

GEOGRAPHY

Area: 5,100,000 sq. mi. (13,209,000 sq km); nearly one-tenth of the earth's land surface

Border: The continent is bounded by the South Atlantic, Indian, and South Pacific Oceans, which join together to form the Southern (or Antarctic) Ocean. The southern tip of South America is more than 600 mi. (966 km) from the Antarctic Peninsula and Australia is 1,550 mi. (2,494 km) from the Ross Ice Shelf.

Coastline: About 19,800 mi. (about 31,900 km)

Dry Valleys: Antarctica's dry valleys rank among the most incredible places on earth. No rain is known to have fallen in these valleys for more than two million years. The extremely dry katabatic winds cause any snow blown into the valleys to evaporate. The Taylor, Victoria, and Wright Valleys are the largest continuous areas of ice-free land on the continent.

Geographic South Pole: The point at which all the south latitudinal lines meet, 90 degrees south, located at an altitude of approximately 9,800 ft. (2,987 m)

Glaciers: Glaciers are created over hundreds of years by densely packed snow. The Lambert Glacier, 248-mi. (399-km) long, is the largest glacier on earth. The fastest-moving glacier is the Shirase; it moves approximately 1.2 mi. (1.9 km) per year. Other glaciers include the Beardmore, Byrd, Rennick, Mackay, David, Priestley, Support Force, Reedy, and Nimrod.

Highest Point: Vinson Massif at 16,859 ft. (5,139 m)

Ice Shelves: The Amery, Filchner, Larsen, Ronne, and Ross ice shelves are found in the Antarctic.

Islands: Antarctic coastal islands include Alexander, Roosevelt, and Ross; Antarctic maritime islands include the Ballenys, South Orkneys, and South Shetlands; and subantarctic islands (near Antarctica) include Heard Island, MacDonald Island, and South Georgia.

Land: Antarctica is the world's coldest, highest, driest, windiest, and fifth-largest continent. Ninety-eight percent of the continent is covered by ice–sometimes as thick as 2 mi. (3 km). Almost all the land is under ice. An area of less than 2 percent along the coast is ice-free. The continent is centered roughly on the geographic South Pole. The shape of the snow-covered land surface is determined by using radio-echo soundings to penetrate the ice.

Lowest Point: In many places the landmass is well below sea level because the weight of the ice pushes the land down.

Mountains: The Transantarctic Mountains are the longest range in Antarctica, stretching 3,000 mi. (4,828 km) from the Ross Sea to the Weddell Sea. Several peaks exceed 14,000 ft. (4,267 m). The mountains divide the continent into two parts: the larger is East (Greater) Antarctica, and the smaller is West (Lesser) Antarctica. Other mountains include the Prince Charles Mountains and Ellsworth Mountains. Antarctica is the earth's highest continent, with an average elevation of 7,500 ft. (2,286 m).

Seas: The two major seas are the Ross and the Weddell.

South Magnetic Pole: The farthest point on earth in the direction of magnetic south; the pole may move 5 to 10 mi. (8 to 16 km) in a year. Magnetic effects are the strongest in this region.

Volcanoes: Mount Erebus at 12,444 ft. (3,793 m) is Antarctica's largest volcano and is still active. Mount Gaussberg is the only volcano in East Antarctica.

Width of Antarctica: The distance between the Antarctic Peninsula to the Wilhelm II Coast measures approximately 3,450 mi. (5,552 km).

BIOLOGY

Birds: More than 40 species of flying birds spend the austral summer in the Antarctic. Dense plumage and body fat protects the birds from the cold. Seabird species include snow petrels, albatrosses, fulmars, dove prions, and terns; shorebirds include blue-eyed cormorants, Dominican gulls, penguins, Antarctic terns, and brown skuas; land birds include wattled sheathbills, penguins, South Georgia pintails, and South Georgia pipits. Banding and recovery studies show that some Antarctic birds travel throughout the world.

Land Animals: The land is too cold and barren to support much life. The native land fauna is wholly invertebrate and includes various life forms, from microscopic single-cell creatures to insects approximately one-half in. (12 mm) long.

Plants: Antarctic plants total approximately 800 species, of which 350 are lichens. Grass and pearlwort grow south of 60° south latitude. Two species of flowering plants grow on Antarctic maritime islands. The most common plants are mosses and lichens along the coast of the continent. Green nonflowering plants called liverworts are found along the Antarctic Peninsula. Life also exists in the form of bacteria, molds, yeasts, algae, and fungi. Tussock grass grows on the subantarctic islands. Fossilized stumps of deciduous trees discovered in Antarctica suggest a much warmer climate occurred during the period just after dinosaurs lived on earth.

Sea Animals: These range from small floating animals called zooplankton (most common is the Antarctic krill) to birds and large mammals. Sea life includes some 100 species of fish, squid, seals, whales, and penguins. There are seven species of penguins–Adélie, chinstrap, emperor, gentoo, king, macaroni, and rockhopper. (Some books claim eight species of penguins occur in Antarctica.) There also are six species of seals–Antarctic fur, crabeater, leopard, Ross, southern elephant, and Weddell. Seals have blubber and dense fur to insulate them from the cold. Great numbers of elephant seals were depleted by hunters who sought their oil, but now seals and whales are protected under international law. Six different species of whales–blue, fin, humpback, minke, sei, and southern right–that belong to the southern baleen whale group make their home in Antarctic waters for at least part of the year. Six different species of toothed whales that are commonly seen in Antarctic waters are sperm, orca (killer), southern bottlenose, southern four-tooth and hourglass, and southern right whale dolphins.

PENGUINS OF ANTARCTICA

Name	Identification	Diet	Average weight and height	Distribution	Breeding
Adélie	solid black head and back, with white eye ring; white front; stubby, dark bill	krill, larval fish	11 lbs. (5 kg) 28 in. (71 cm)	shores around Antarctica, and some Antarctic islands	lays 2 eggs* that take 36 days to hatch; nests made of scattered piles of pebbles
Chinstrap	only top and back of head is black, like a cap that is held on by a thin black strap around the chin; slender black bill; pale pink feet	krill	10 lbs. (4.5 kg) 30 in. (76 cm)	Antarctic Peninsula (western shore), islands north of Antarctica in the Atlantic Ocean	lays 2 eggs* that take 37 days to hatch; nests made of a a platform of pebbles
Emperor	blue-gray back; yellow or orange patches on the side of its head and neck and a lemon-yellow breast	krill, larval fish	66 lbs. (30 kg) 42 in. (106 cm)	below the Antarctic Convergence on continental Antarctica	lays 1 egg that is incubated on the feet; takes 9 weeks to hatch; no nest, egg is laid on ice; breed in winter
Gentoo	white "ear-muff" band across the head from one eye to the other; yellow bill; yellow-orange feet	krill, fish, squid	12-13 lbs. (5.5-6 kg) 27 in. (71 cm)	Antarctic Peninsula and subantarctic islands as far north as 52 degrees	lays 2 eggs* that hatch in 36 days; nests made of stones, moss, and seaweed
King	blue-gray jacket; long beak; yellow chest; deep orange collar or neck patches	squid, fish	33 lbs. (15 kg) 36 in. (91 cm)	Antarctic and subantarctic islands to the tip of South America	lays 1 egg, which is incubated on the feet covered by a flap of skin; takes 6-6½ weeks to hatch; no nest
Macaroni	orange-yellow plumes grow from forehead on each side of its head	krill	10 lbs. (4.5 kg) 28 in. (71 cm)	subantarctic islands in the Atlantic and Indian Oceans	lays 2 eggs* that take 36 days to hatch; nests made of available material (twigs)
Rockhopper	small red eyes; yellow eyebrows; golden plumes on each side of its head; orange bill; pink feet	krill	5.5 lbs. (2.5 kg) 22 in. (56 cm)	subantarctic islands and Antarctica	lays 2 eggs* that take 35 days to hatch; nests made of available material (twigs)

*often only 1 survives

SEALS OF ANTARCTICA

Species	Identification	Diet	Average weight and height	Distribution
Weddell	short head and snout, silver-gray coat spotted with black, gray, and white	fish	880 lbs. (400 kg) 10 ft. (3 m)	farthest south of all species, found on fast ice near Antarctic coast
Ross	wide head, very short snout, very large eyes, tan colored body with dark brown hind limbs and top of head	mostly squid, some fish and krill	440 lbs. (200 kg) 7.5 ft. (2.3 m)	western pack ice around the continent
Crabeater	dark gray along spine with tan colored sides and belly	mostly krill, some fish and squid	550 lbs. (250 kg) 8.8 ft. (2.7 m)	drifting pack ice around the continent
Leopard	shades of gray from dark along the spine to pale on the belly; noticeable spots on head, neck, and sides; long sinuous body with long reptilianlike head	penguins, krill, fish, and squid	770 lbs. (350 kg) 10 ft. (3 m)	northern edge of the pack ice throughout the Southern Ocean
Southern Elephant	males are grayish brown; females are brown; mature males have an inflatable trunk or proboscis	fish, squid, octopus, and crustaceans	males, up to 4 tons, (2,484 kg), 20-23 ft. (6-7 m); females, 1 ton (609 kg), 10-13 ft. (3-4 m)	subantarctic islands
Antarctic Fur	dark gray along spine with yellow throat and chest; brown back and flippers, males have heavy mane around neck and shoulders, use limbs to get around, true ear	fish, crustaceans	males, 220 lbs. (100 kg) 7 ft. (2 m); females, 110 lbs. (50 kg) 5 ft. (1.5 m)	north and south of the Antarctic Convergence, primarily on subantarctic islands, mostly South Georgia

ECONOMY AND INDUSTRY

Fishing: Commercial fishing and krill harvesting take place off the Antarctic coast.

Mining: Antarctica may have resources such as coal, iron, copper, gold, platinum, nickel, oil, and natural gas. Mineral exploration has been limited to comparatively small ice-free areas. The ecosystems of Antarctica may be extremely fragile. The 1991 Protocol on Environmental Protection, part of the Antarctic Treaty System, bans all exploration and mining of natural resources on the continent for at least fifty years to protect the ecosystem.

Tourism: Antarctica offers many tourist attractions, including wildlife, ice and snow, beautiful scenery, historic monuments, and remote wilderness. Most tourists arrive aboard cruise ships. Tourism is steadily increasing. Most tour operators and tourists follow agreed-on guidelines while in Antarctica.

Transportation: Aircraft are used routinely to carry both passengers and priority supplies to some research stations. Transport between stations in the interior is provided mainly by tractor trains and ski-equipped aircraft. Transportation costs are very expensive because icebreakers and specially equipped airplanes are needed.

THE ANTARCTIC TREATY

Antarctic Treaty: The treaty is an international agreement designed to regulate human activity in Antarctica. As of 1994 forty-two nations are bound by the treaty, but any nation can decide to withdraw. The treaty calls for international cooperation and freedom of scientific investigation and bans any military activity, weapons testing, nuclear testing, and disposal of radioactive waste in the region. There are four official treaty languages: English, French, Russian, and Spanish.

Antarctic Treaty System (ATS): The collective body of agreements governing Antarctica, including the Antarctic Treaty; all recommendations made since the treaty entered into force; and supplementary instruments such as the Agreed Measures, the Convention for the Conservation of Antarctic Seals, the Convention on the Conservation of Antarctic Marine Living Resources, the Protocol on Environmental Protection, and recommendations enacted by treaty parties to cover Antarctic activities.

Signatories to the Antarctic Treaty: The twelve original treaty signatories in 1959 included Argentina, Australia, Belgium, Chile, France, Japan, New Zealand, Norway, South Africa, the USSR, the United Kingdom, and the United States. Further signatories of the Antarctic Treaty include Austria, Brazil, Bulgaria, Canada, the People's Republic of China, Colombia, Cuba, the Czech Republic, Denmark, Ecuador, Finland, Germany, Greece, Guatemala, Hungary, India, Italy, the Democratic People's Republic of Korea, the Republic of Korea, the Netherlands, Papua New Guinea, Peru, Poland, Romania, the Republic of Slovakia, Spain, Sweden, Switzerland, Ukraine, and Uruguay.

Antarctic Treaty nations have either consultative or nonconsultative status. Consultative parties have voting rights. To become a consultative party, and thereby obtain full voting rights, a nation must show significant interest in the region by conducting scientific research. If a nation wishes to participate in the Antarctic Treaty System, but does not have a science program in the Antarctic, it must accept the agreements of the ATS. Nonconsultative parties are those nations that have signed the Antarctic Treaty, which means that they will abide by the treaty regulations, but have not yet sponsored a significant scientific program in Antarctica. Setting up a research program in Antarctica is necessary to obtain consultative status.

Consultative Parties (26): Argentina, Australia, Belgium, Brazil, Chile, the People's Republic of China, Ecuador, Finland, France, Germany, India, Italy, Japan, the Republic of Korea, the Netherlands, New Zealand, Norway, Peru, Poland, Russia, South Africa, Spain, Sweden, the United Kingdom, the United States of America, and Uruguay

Nonconsultative Parties (16): Austria, Bulgaria, Canada, Colombia, Cuba, the Czech Republic, Denmark, Greece, Guatemala, Hungary, the Democratic People's Republic of Korea, Papua New Guinea, Romania, the Republic of Slovakia, Switzerland, and Ukraine

Nongovernmental Organizations and Conservation Groups: Among the most active nongovernmental organizations in Antarctic affairs are Greenpeace, The Antarctica Project, and the International Union for Conservation of Nature and Natural Resources (IUCN). A coalition of over 200 nongovernmental organizations around the world—the Antarctic and Southern Ocean coalition—monitors compliance with the Antarctic Treaty System and attends all meetings of the Antarctic Treaty as an expert adviser on the environment.

Research Stations: Many Antarctic Treaty countries have established Antarctic research stations specializing in fields such as biology, geology, meteorology, and physics. The following research stations were in operation south of 60° south latitude in Antarctica during the winter of 1992:

Argentina: Belgrano II, Esperanza, Jubany, Marambio, Orcadas, San Martín

Australia: Casey, Davis, Mawson

Brazil: Commandante Ferraz

Chile: Capitan Arturo Prat, General Bernardo O'Higgins, Teniente Rodolfo Marsh

People's Republic of China: Great Wall, Zhongshan

France: Dumont d'Urville

Germany: Georg von Neumayer

India: Maitri

Japan: Syowa, Asuka

Republic of Korea: King Sejong

New Zealand: Scott Base

Poland: Arctowski

Russia: Bellingshausen, Mirny, Molodezhnaya, Novolazarevskaya, Vostok (the second-largest station in Antarctica)

South Africa: SANAE

United Kingdom: Faraday, Halley V, Rothera, Signy

United States: McMurdo (the largest station in Antarctica), Palmer, Amundsen-Scott South Pole Station

Uruguay: Artigas

IMPORTANT DATES

1773–Captain James Cook crosses the Antarctic Circle while searching for the southern continent

1820–The Antarctic continent is sighted for the first time

1821–John Davis makes the first landing on Antarctica

1822–James Weddell launches a sealing expedition in southern waters with two ships

1823–Weddell lands in the South Orkneys

1840–French d'Urville expedition crosses the Antarctic Circle and sights Antarctica

1841–English expedition under James Clark Ross explores and names Mount Erebus and discovers what is now called the Ross Ice Shelf

1875–Karl Weyprecht, an Austrian naval officer, proposes that all scientific programs in both the Arctic and Antarctic be coordinated

1882-83–The first International Polar Year takes place

1895–Henryk Johan Bull's party makes the first confirmed landing on the Antarctic continent outside the Antarctic Peninsula

1902–Swedish explorer Otto Nordenskjöld covers 400 mi. (644 km) in 33 days; British *Discovery* expedition to Antarctica is headed by Robert Falcon Scott and includes Ernest Shackleton

1904-66–South Georgia is home to the largest whaling station in the area

1908–The United Kingdom claims territory in Antarctica; Shackleton leads an expedition to Antarctica

1909–Edgeworth David, Douglas Mawson, and Alistair Mackay reach the South Magnetic Pole

1911–Robert F. Scott arrives at McMurdo Sound to establish a base camp from which to attempt to reach the South Pole; Amundsen arrives at the Bay of Whales to set out for the South Pole; Amundsen becomes the first person to reach the South Pole

1912–Robert F. Scott arrives at the South Pole; Scott and his four companions die on the return journey

1914–Sir Ernest Shackleton leads the Imperial Trans-Antarctic Expedition to Antarctica

1915–Shackleton's ship, the *Endurance*, is crushed in the ice of the Weddell Sea

1916–Shackleton and five companions brave stormy seas to reach South Georgia to launch a rescue attempt of twenty-two expedition members stranded on Elephant Island

1923–New Zealand claims territory in Antarctica

1924–France claims territory in Antarctica

1928–The first plane flies over Antarctica; Richard Byrd leads a U.S. Antarctic expedition; Byrd establishes Little America Base, Bay of Whales

1932-33–The second International Polar Year takes place

1933–Australia claims territory in Antarctica

1934–Byrd is the first person to spend a winter in the Antarctic interior, but nearly dies of carbon monoxide poisoning

1935–Ellsworth makes the first successful trans-Antarctic flight; Caroline Mikkelsen is the first woman to step on the Antarctic continent, at the Vestfold Hills

1939–Norway claims territory in Antarctica

1940–Chile claims territory in Antarctica

1942–Argentina claims territory in Antarctica

1946-47–The United States navy conducts Operation Highjump with 4,700 men, 13 ships, and 23 airplanes to map extensive coastal areas using aerial photography

1947–Icebreakers are used for the first time in Antarctica; Edith Ronne and Jennie Darlington are the first women to live and work in Antarctica, spending nearly a year on Stonington Island near the Antarctic Peninsula

1952–Ship log of John Davis is discovered

1955–Representatives from twelve nations, planning research in the Antarctic during the International Geophysical Year (IGY), meet in Paris

1956–Airlines first fly tourist groups over the Antarctic continent

1957-58–Twelve nations conduct research in Antarctica during the International Geophysical Year; the United States builds research facilities in Antarctica, including a large support station at McMurdo Sound, Byrd Station in Marie Byrd Land, Ellsworth Station on the Filchner Ice Shelf, and Amundsen-Scott South Pole Station; the Soviet Union builds a station at the Pole of Inaccessibility, the farthest point from all Antarctic coasts

1958–The first overland continental crossing is completed by Vivian Fuchs

1959–The Antarctic Treaty is signed by the twelve nations involved in Antarctic research during the IGY: Argentina, Australia, Belgium, Chile, France, Japan, New Zealand, Norway, South Africa, the United Kingdom, the United States, and the Soviet Union

1961–The Antarctic Treaty enters into force

1967–Volcanic eruption starts on Deception Island (ends in 1970)

1979–An Air New Zealand DC-10 crashes into Mount Erebus, killing all 257 passengers and crew

1983–The lowest temperature ever recorded in Antarctica is taken at Vostok Station, -129.3° F. (-89.6° C)

1987–British scientists first discover a "hole" in the ozone layer over Antarctica

1990–The United Kingdom builds an airstrip at Rothera Station

1991–The treaty parties sign the Protocol on Environmental Protection to the Antarctic Treaty (part of the Antarctic Treaty System), designed to preserve the unique environment in Antarctica

1991-92–Approximately 6,500 tourists visit Antarctica during the 1992-93 austral summer

1993–Geophysicists Donald Blankenship and Robin Bell discover evidence of several active volcanoes beneath the West Antarctic ice sheet; approximately 7,200 tourists visit Antarctica during the austral summer; in a joint effort by NASA and the United States Antarctic Program (USAP), Antarctica is selected as a test site for equipment destined for use on the moon and Mars; NASA sends an eight-legged robot named Dante into Mount Erebus, an active volcano; Norwegian lawyer Erling Kagge becomes the first person to walk unaccompanied to the South Pole, making a 51-day, 814-mi. (1,310-km) journey

1994–The International Whaling Commission creates a sanctuary around Antarctica, putting nearly one-quarter of the world's oceans off-limits to commercial whaling

IMPORTANT PEOPLE

Roald Amundsen (1872-1928), Norwegian explorer; the first person to reach the South Pole in 1911; named the Queen Maud Mountains and King Haakon VII Plateau; writings include *North West Passage* (1908), *The South Pole* (1912), and *My Life as an Explorer* (1927)

Admiral Fabian von Bellingshausen (1778-1852), Russian explorer; possibly the first person to sight the Antarctic continent; the Bellingshausen Sea is named after him

Carsten Egeberg Borchgrevink (1864-1934), Norwegian naturalist and explorer; established a base at McMurdo Sound; made the first sled journey on the Ross Ice Shelf

Edward Bransfield (c. 1795-1852), English explorer and naval officer; on January 30, 1820, was the first to sight the Antarctic Peninsula; first to chart a portion of the Antarctic mainland

Henryk Johan Bull (1844-1930), Norwegian explorer; made the first landing on the Antarctic continent outside the peninsula at Cape Adare

Richard Evelyn Byrd (1888-1957), U.S. naval officer, polar aviator, and explorer; the first person to fly over the North Pole in 1926 and the South Pole in 1929; named the Rockefeller Mountains; led a U.S. expedition from 1939 to 1941 and later headed Operation Highjump from 1946 to 1947; was in charge of Operation Deepfreeze in 1955 and 1956

James Cook (1728-79), also known as Captain Cook; English mariner and explorer; was the first to cross the Antarctic Circle; circumnavigated Antarctica

Jennie Darlington, one of the two women researchers who were the first to spend a year living and working in the Antarctic; both were accompanied by their husbands.

Sir Edgeworth David (1858-1934), British-born Australian geologist; was the first to reach the South Magnetic Pole with two companions; author of *The Geology of Australia* (1932)

Captain John Davis, U.S. sealer; in 1821 possibly the first person to set foot on the Antarctic mainland

Jules-Sebastien-Cesar Dumont d'Urville (1790-1842), French naval commander and explorer; led an expedition to Antarctica from 1837 to 1840

Lincoln Ellsworth (1880-1951), U.S. explorer; with Herbert Hollick-Kenyon made the first flight across the continent of Antarctica; Ellsworth Land is named after him

Sir Vivian Ernest Fuchs (1908-), English explorer; leader of the Commonwealth Trans-Antarctic Expedition; completed the first overland continental crossing; co-authored *The Crossing of Antarctica* (1958)

Sir Edmund Hillary (1919-), New Zealand explorer; pioneered a new route onto the polar plateau; led first ascent of Mt. Herschel

Sir Douglas Mawson (1882-1958), Australian explorer and geologist; led an expedition to Commonwealth Bay from 1911 to 1914; discovered MacRobertson Land, the Banzare Coast, and Princess Elizabeth Land

Nils Otto Gustaf Nordenskjöld (1869-1928), Swedish explorer and geographer; led the Swedish South Polar Expedition, 1901-04

Nathaniel Brown Palmer (1799-1877), U.S. explorer and sealer; Palmer Land is named after him

Edith Ronne (c. 1915-), wife of Finn Ronne; one of two women researchers who were the first to spend a year living and working in the Antarctic, accompanied by their husbands; the Ronne Ice Shelf was originally named Edith Ronne Land

Captain Finn Ronne (1899-1980), U.S. explorer; led a private expedition to West Antarctica by air; the Ronne Ice Shelf is named after him

Sir James Clark Ross (1800-62), Scottish explorer; discovered the Ross Sea, the Admiralty Mountains, and Victoria Land; the Ross Ice Shelf is named after him

Robert Falcon Scott (1868-1912), English explorer; led the British *Discovery* expedition from 1901 to 1904; explored and named King Edward VII Land; reached the South Pole in 1912 after Amundsen; died with companions on return journey to their base camp

Sir Ernest Henry Shackleton (1874-1922), British explorer; led an Antarctic

A British expedition uses skidoos for transportation.

expedition from 1907-09; he and his crew survived the loss of their ship, the *Endurance*, during a 1914-16 Antarctic expedition; won fame and was knighted by King Edward VII of England

Paul Allman Siple (1908-68), American naturalist and geographer; chosen as a Boy Scout to accompany Byrd on his first Antarctic expedition, 1928 to 1930, the first of many trips south; spent the first winter at the South Pole as scientific leader

William Smith (c. 1790-1834), British mariner; discovered the South Shetland Islands in 1819; later discovered the northwestern coast of the Antarctic Peninsula with Edward Bransfield

James Weddell (1787-1834), English sealer, navigator, and explorer; the Weddell Sea and Weddell seal are named after him

Charles Wilkes (1798-1877), U.S. naval officer and explorer; his expedition explored 1,240 mi. (1,996 km) of East Antarctica's coastline; Wilkes Land is named after him

Sir George Hubert Wilkins (1888-1958), Australian explorer and aviator; made the first Antarctic flight

Compiled by Chandrika Kaul

INDEX

Page numbers that appear in boldface type indicate illustrations

Adams, Jameson, 60, **76**
Adéle's Land, 55
Admiralty Mountains, 57, 120
Africa, 13
Agreed Measures for the
    Conservation of Antarctic
    Fauna and Flora, 92, 113
albatross, 43, **43**, 110
Alexander Island, 24, 109
algae, 36, **36**, 110
Amery Ice Shelf, 19, 109
Amundsen, Roald, 62-63, 64, **64**,
    66-67, 69-70, 71, 72, 78, 81, 89,
    119
    route to South Pole, **65**
Amundsen-Scott South Pole
    Station, 99, **99**, 118
animals, **4, 5,** 36-37, 110
Antarctic, 58
Antarctic Circle, 10, 15, 54, 115
Antarctic coastal islands, 24, 109
Antarctic Convergence, 15-16, **15,**
    21, 25, 43, 106
Antarctic maritime islands, 24-25,
    109
Antarctic Ocean, 13-14
Antarctic Peninsula, 14, **20, 26,**
    30, 33, 35, **36,** 54, 58, 78, 86,
    106, 109, 110, 116, 117
Antarctic terns, 43, 110
Antarctic Treaty (1959), 16, 90-92,
    108, 113-115, 118
Arctic Ocean, 29
Arctic region, 29
Arctowski Station, **100**
area, 7, 108
Argentina, Antarctic claims of,
    108, 117
Argentina, research in
    Antarctica, 88, 100
Argentina, signatory to Antarctic
    Treaty, 118
Aristotle, 7, **8**
Asia, 17
Astrolabe, 54
Atlantic Ocean, 13, 15, 106
Australia, Antarctic claims of,
    86-87, 108

Australia, research and
    exploration in Antarctica, 62,
    82-83, 88, 100, 115
Australia, signatory to Antarctic
    Treaty, 114, 118
Austria, signatory to Antarctic
    Treaty, 114
Axel Heiberg Glacier, 80
bacteria, 36, 110
Balchen, Bernt, 80
baleen, 48
Balleny Islands, 24, 109
Banzare Coast, 83, 120
Bay of Whales, 65, 67, 68, 79, 83,
    116, 117
Beardmore Glacier, 19, 60, 68, 69,
    108
Beaufoy, 54
Belgium, Antarctic claims of, 86,
    108
Belgium, research and
    exploration in Antarctica, 86, 88
Belgium, signatory to Antarctic
    Treaty, 114, 118
Bell, Robin, 119
Bellingshausen, Fabian von, 11,
    16, 52, 119
Bellingshausen Sea, 16
Berkner, Lloyd, 87
birds, 42-43, **43,** 110
Bjaaland, Olav Olavsen, 67
Blankenship, Donald, 119
blizzards, 31-33, **32,** 68, 69, 70, 71,
    94, 106
Bolling Advance Weather Station,
    81
Borchgrevink, Carsten Egeberg,
    119
borders, 108
Bowers, Henry, 68, 69
Bransfield, Edward, 52, 119, 121
Brazil, research in Antarctica,
    100, 115
Brazil, signatory to Antarctic
    Treaty, 114
brown skuas, 43, **43,** 110
Bulgaria, signatory to Antarctic
    Treaty, 114

Bull, Henryk Johan, 58, 116, 119
Byrd, Richard Evelyn, 78-82, **78,** 80, **81,** 117, 119
Byrd Glacier, 19, 108
Byrd Station, 89, 118
calving, 20-21, 106
Canada, signatory to Antarctic Treaty, 114
Cape Adare, 58, 119
Cape Charles, 53
Cape Evans, 70
Cape Hallett, **6**
Cape Royds, 60, **73**
Cecilia, 53
Chile, Antarctic claims of, 108, 117
Chile, research in Antarctica, 88, 100, 115
Chile, signatory to Antarctic Treaty, 114, 118
China, research in Antarctica, 100, 115
China, signatory to Antarctic Treaty, 114
carbons, 98
climate, 27-33, 106
coast, 13, 108
Columbia, signatory to Antarctic Treaty, 114
Columbus, Christopher, 9, **9**
Comite Special de l'Annee Geophysique Internationale (CSAGI), 88
Commonwealth Bay, 31, 106
Commonwealth of Independent States (CIS), 108
Commonwealth Trans-Antarctic expedition, 83-84, 120
Convention for the Conservation of Antarctic Seals (CCAS), 92, 113
Convention on the Conservation of Antarctic Marine Living Resources (CCAMLR), 92, 113
Cook, James, 10, 115, 119
cormorant, 43, **43,** 110
Crean, Tom, 76
Cuba, signatory to Antarctic Treaty, 114
cyclones, 33, 106

Czech Republic, signatory to Antarctic Treaty, 114
da Gama, Vasco, 9, **9**
Dante, 119
Darlington, Jennie, 84, 117, 119
David, Edgeworth, 60, 82, 116, 120
David Glacier, 108
Davis, John, 52-53, 116, 118, 120
Davis Station, **90**
Deception Island, 77, 118
de la Roche, Antonio, 10
de Lozier, Jean-Baptiste Charles Bouvet, 10
Denmark, signatory to Antarctic Treaty, 114
Discovery, 116
dolphins, 110
Dominican gulls, 43, 110
dove prions, 43, 110
Drake, Francis, 10, **10**
dry valleys, 22-23, **23,** 108
Dundee Island, 83
d'Urville, Jules-Sébastien-César Dumont, 54, 116, 120
East (Greater) Antarctica, 14-15, **15,** 16, 20, 109
Ecuador, signatory to Antarctic Treaty, 114
Edith Ronne Land, 84, 120
Edward VII, 61
Elephant Island, 74, 76, 117
elevation, 17, 19, 109
Ellsworth, Lincoln, 83, **83,** 117, 120
Ellsworth Land, 83, 120
Ellsworth Mountains, 22, 109
Ellsworth Station, 89, 118
Endurance, 72, 73-74, 77, 117
environment, 98-100, **98, 99, 100**
Environmental Defense Fund, 92, 114
Erebus, 56, 57
Evans, Edgar, 68
Filchner Ice Shelf, 19, 89, 109, 118
Finland, signatory to Antarctic Treaty, 114
fishing, 36-37, 93, 110, 113
flag, 107
Flag Research Center, 107

France, Antarctic claims of, 86, 108, 117

France, research and exploration in Antarctica, 54-55, 88, 100, 115

France, signatory to Antarctic Treaty, 114, 118

frostbite, 28

Fuchs, Vivian Ernest, 83-84, **83,** 88, 118, 120

fungi, 36, 110

geographic South Pole, 59, 64, 108

geography, 7, 108

George V Coast, 31

George V Land, 82

Germany, Antarctic claims of, 86

Germany, research and exploration in Antarctica, 62, 100, 115

Germany, signatory to Antarctic Treaty, 114

glaciers, 19-20, **22,** 108

global warming, 98-99

Gondwana, 14, **14**

Gore, Al, 101

Graham Land, 86

grass, 34-35, 110

Great Britain, Antarctic claims of, 116

Great Britain, exploration in Antarctica, 54, 56-57, 59-61, 62

Greece, signatory to Antarctic Treaty, 114

Greenpeace, 92, 114

Guatemala, signatory to Antarctic Treaty, 114

Haakon VII, 70

Hanssen, Helmer Julius, 67

Hassel, Helge Sverre, 67

Heard Island, 25, 40, 109

Henson, Matthew, 62, 63, **63**

Hillary, Edmund, 120

history, 52-92, 115-119

Hollick-Kenyon, Herbert, 83, **83,** 120

Hope Bay, **20**

Hungary, signatory to Antarctic Treaty, 114

huskies, 66, **66**

icebergs, 20-21, **20, 21**

ice cover, 16-17, **18,** 19

ice sheet, 19

ice shelves, **18,** 19, 107, 109

Imperial Trans-Antarctic Expedition, 117

India, research in Antarctica, 100, 115

India, signatory to Antarctic Treaty, 114

Indian Ocean, 13, 15, 106

International Council of Scientific Unions (ICSU), 87-88

International Court of Justice, 91

International Geophysical Year (IGY), 16, 88, 89, 90, 118

International Polar Years, 87, 116, 117

International Union for Conservation of Nature and Natural Resources (IUCN), 114

islands, 24-25, 109

Italy, signatory to Antarctic Treaty, 114

James Caird, 74

Jane, 54

Japan, Antarctic claims of, 86, 108

Japan, research and exploration in Antarctica, 62, 88, 100, 115

Japan, signatory to Antarctic Treaty, 114, 118

June, Harold, 80

katabatic winds, 31, 107

King Edward VII Land, 64, 120

King Haakon VII Plateau, 67, 119

Korea, the People's Republic of, signatory to Antarctic Treaty, 114

Korea, the Republic of, research in Antarctica, 100, 115

Korea, the Republic of, signatory to Antarctic Treaty, 114

krill, 37, **37,** 110, 113

Lambert Glacier, 20, 108

land, 109

Larsen Ice Shelf, 109

lichens, 35, **35**

Little America, 79, 80, 83, 117

liverworts, 35, 110

Liv Glacier, 80

Low Islands, 53

MacDonald Island, 25, 109
Mackay, Alistair, 60, 116
Mackay Glacier, 108
MacRobertson Land, 83, 120
Magellan, Ferdinand, 9-10, **10**
maps
  political, **104**
  regional, **1**
  topographical, **2**
Marie Byrd Land, 89, 118
Marshall, Eric, 60, **76**
Mawson, Douglas, 60, 82-83, **82,**
  116, 120
McKinley, Ashley, 80
McMurdo Sound, 65, 68, 89, **89,**
  99, 116, 118, 119
McMurdo Station, **89,** 99, **99,** 107,
  115
Mikkelsen, Caroline, 84, 117
mineral resources, 93-94, 113
molds, 110
mosses, 35, **35**
mountains, **17,** 22, **22,** 109
Mount Erebus, 24, **24,** 57, **60, 61,**
  82, 109, 116, 118, 119
Mount Gaussberg, 109
Mount Herschel, 120
Mount Terror, 57
National Aeronautics and Space
  Administration (NASA), 24, 119
national expeditions, 54-57
Netherlands, the, signatory to
  Antarctic Treaty, 114
New Zealand, Antarctic claims of,
  86, 108, 117
New Zealand, research in
  Antarctica, 88, 100, 115
New Zealand, signatory to
  Antarctic Treaty, 114, 118
Nimrod, 59, **59,** 60
Nimrod Glacier, 19, 108
Nordenskjöld, Nils Otto Gustaf,
  58, 116, 120
North Pole, 29
Norway, Antarctic claims of, 86,
  108, 117
Norway, research and
  exploration in Antarctica, 58,
  62, 66-67, 88
Norway, signatory to Antarctic
  Treaty, 114, 118

nunataks, 17, **17,** 107
Oates, Lawrence, 68, 70
O'Higgins, Bernardo, 86
O'Higgins Land, 86
Operation Deepfreeze, 82, 119
Operation Highjump, 81-82, **81,**
  117, 119
ozone hole, 98, **98,** 107
ozone layer, 118
Pacific Ocean, 13, 15, 106
pack ice, 107
Palmer, Nathaniel Brown, 16, 52,
  53, 86, 120
Palmer Land, 16, 86, 120
Palmer Peninsula, 86
Papua New Guinea, signatory to
  Antarctic Treaty, 114
Paradise Bay, **26**
Paulet Island, 59
pearlworts, 34-35, 110
Peary, Robert E., 62, 63, **63**
penguins, **4, 5,** 25, **25,** 37, 38, **39,**
  40-42, **40, 41, 42,** 95, **95, 102,**
  110, 111
  chart of Antarctic penguins, **111**
Peru, signatory to Antarctic
  Treaty, 114
phytoplankton, 37
plants, 34-36, **35, 36,** 110
Poland, research in Antarctica,
  100, 115
Poland, signatory to Antarctic
  Treaty, 114
Pole of Inaccessibility, 118
pollution, 107
population, 107
Porpoise, 55
precipitation, 33, 106
Priestley Glacier, 108
Prince Charles Mountains, 16, 20,
  109
Princess Elizabeth Land, 83, 120
Protocol on Environmental
  Protection, 92, 113, 118
Ptolemy, 8, **8**
Queen Maud Land, 16, 20
Queen Maud Mountains, 67, 80,
  119
Quest, 77
Reedy Glacier, 108
Rennick Glacier, 108

research stations, 114-115
Rockefeller Mountains, 79, 119
Romania, signatory to Antarctic
    Treaty, 114
Ronne, Edith, 84, 117, 120
Ronne, Finn, 120
Ronne Ice Shelf, 19, 84, 109, 120
Roosevelt Island, 24, 109
Ross, James Clark, 16, 56-57, **56,**
    116, 120
Ross Ice Shelf, 16, **18,** 19, 57, 65,
    68, 79, 80, 108, 109, 116, 120
Ross Island, 24, **24,** 109
Ross Sea, **6,** 14, 22, 57, 72, 109,
    120
Rothera Station, 118
Russia, research in Antarctica,
    100, 115
San Martín, José de, 86
San Martín Land, 86
sastrugi, 32, **32**
Scientific Committee on Antarctic
    Research (SCAR), 90
scientific research, 94-95, **94,** 96,
    98, 99-100, 118
Scott, Kathleen, 84
Scott, Robert Falcon, 59, 62, 63,
    64-65, **64,** 67-69, **68,** 70-71, **71,**
    81, 84, 89, 116, 120
    route to South Pole, **65**
seabirds, 25, 95
seals, 10, 23, 37, **44,** 46, **46,** 47, **47,**
    54, 95, 110
    chart of Antarctic seals, **112**
seas, 109
Sentinel Range, 22
Shackleton, Emily, 84, 116
Shackleton, Ernest Henry, 59-61,
    59, 60, 72-77, **76,** 84, 85, 116,
    117, 120-121
sheathbills, 43, 110
Shirase, 20, 108
Siberian ponies, 60-61, 66, 67, 69
Siple, Paul Allman, 121
Smith, William, 53, 121
Smith Island, 53
Snow Hill Island, 58, 59
snow petrels, 43, **43,** 110
solar radiation, 29
South Africa, Antarctic claims of,
    88, 108

South Africa, research in
    Antarctica, 100, 115
South Africa, signatory to
    Antarctic Treaty, 114, 118
South America, 13
southern giant fulmar, 43, 110
southern lights, 88
Southern Ocean, 16, 33, 106
South Georgia, 25, 40, 74, 75, **75,**
    76, 87, 109, 116
South Georgia pintails, 43, 110
South Georgia pipits, 43, 110
South Magnetic Pole, 13, 57, 59,
    60, 79, 82, 89, 109, 116
South Orkney Island, 24, 54, 86,
    109, 116
South Pole, 13, 29, 30, 80, 89, 106
South Shetland Island, 24, 53,
    109, 121
Soviet Union, Antarctic claims of,
    86-87, 108
Soviet Union, research in
    Antarctica, 89
Soviet Union, signatory to
    Antarctic Treaty, 114, 118
Spain, signatory to Antarctic
    Treaty, 114
square miles, 7, 108
squid, 110
Stonington Island, 84, 117
subantarctic islands, 25, 109
Support Force, 108
Sweden, exploration in
    Antarctica, 58-59
Sweden, signatory to Antarctic
    Treaty, 114
Switzerland, signatory to
    Antarctic Treaty, 114
Taylor Valley, 22, 108
temperatures, 30-31, 106, 118
Terra Australis Incognita, 7-8
Terra Nova, 64, 64
Terror, 56, 57
tourism, 93, 94-97, **95, 96, 97,** 113,
    118
Transantarctic Mountains, **6,**
    14-15, 22, **22, 101,** 109
transportation, 113
tussock grass, 25, 110
Ukraine, signatory to Antarctic
    Treaty, 114

United Kingdom, Antarctic
claims of, 86, 108
United Kingdom, research in
Antarctica, 88, 100, 115, 118
United Kingdom, signatory to
Antarctic Treaty, 114, 118
United States, Antarctic claims
of, 87, 108
United States, research and
exploration in Antarctica, 54-56,
78-82, 88, 115, 117, 118
United States, signatory to
Antarctic Treaty, 114, 118
United States Antarctic Program
(USAP), 100, 119
United States National Science
Foundation (NSF), 99-100
Uruguay, signatory to Antarctic
Treaty, 100, 114, 115
Van Allen, James, 87
Victoria Land, **6,** 16, 57, 120
Victoria Valley, 22, 108
Vinson Massif, 22, 109
volcanoes, 24, **24,** 57, 109, 118
Vostok, 11
Vostok Station, 106
Weddell, James, 54, 116, 121

Weddell Sea, 14, 22, 72-73, 83,
109, 117
West (Lesser) Antarctica, 14-15,
15, 16, 109, 119
Weyprecht, Karl, 87, 116
whales, 10, 48-50, **48, 49, 50, 51,**
95, 110
whaling stations, 25, **75**
White Desert, 33
Wild, Frank, 60, 74, 75, **76,** 77
Wilhelm II Coast, 109
Wilkes, Charles, 55-56, **56,** 121
Wilkes Land, 56, 121
Wilkins, Hubert, 77-78, **78,** 121
Wilson, Edward, 68
wind-chill factor, 27, 28
winds, 27-28, 31, 109
Winter Quarters Bay, 107
Wisting, Oscar, 67
World War I, 85
World War II, 85
Worsley, Frank, 76, 77
Wright Valley, 22, **23,** 108
yeasts, 110
Yelcho, 77
Zélée, 54
zooplankton, 36, 37

About the Author

Henry Billings is a freelance writer of educational materials. He received a B.B.A. from the University of Massachusetts in Amherst, an M.A.T. from Salem State College in Salem, Massachusetts, and completed advanced graduate studies at the University of Massachusetts in educational philosophy.

A high school history teacher for sixteen years, Mr. Billings began his writing career as a freelance journalist specializing in feature articles and humorous op-ed pieces. Along with his wife Melissa, he has written more than fifty textbooks and reading development books since 1984 for such publishers as Steck Vaughn, Jamestown, and Curriculum Associates. In addition, Mr. Billings has written a hardcover high school economics textbook—*Introduction to Economics*—for EMC and a softcover economics text for at-risk students—*Economics: It's Your Business*—for People's Publishing Group. His two humorous trade paperbacks were published by New England Press.